J. R. (John Richardson) Illingworth

Sermons preached in a college chapel

With an appendix

J. R. (John Richardson) Illingworth

Sermons preached in a college chapel

With an appendix

ISBN/EAN: 9783337085865

Printed in Europe, USA, Canada, Australia, Japan

Cover: Foto ©Lupo / pixelio.de

More available books at **www.hansebooks.com**

SERMONS

SERMONS

PREACHED IN A COLLEGE CHAPEL

WITH AN APPENDIX

BY

J. R. ILLINGWORTH, M.A.

FELLOW OF JESUS COLLEGE, AND
TUTOR OF KEBLE COLLEGE, OXFORD.

London
MACMILLAN & CO.
1881

Printed by R. & R. CLARK, *Edinburgh.*

PREFACE.

THE desire of friends whose judgment I was bound to respect above my own has caused the publication of the following Sermons, and of their Appendix, a paper read originally before an Oxford Society, and which was thought not wholly incongruous with the subject of the Sermons.

CONTENTS.

		PAGE
I.	Death	1
II.	Trouble	18
III.	Eternity	32
IV.	The Consequences of Sin	48
V.	Life	60
VI.	The Commination Service	77
VII.	Penitence	90
VIII.	Knowledge	105
IX.	Faith	116
X.	Love	130
XI.	Gathering of Fragments	141
	Appendix	157

I.

DEATH.

"I am He that liveth, and was dead; and, behold, I am alive for evermore, Amen; and have the keys of hell and of death."— REV. i. 18.

DEATH has been called scoffingly the preacher's commonplace; but a commonplace truth, like a commonplace person, is often only a name for one with whose appearance we are very familiar, and whose character we are too indolent to probe. It is a phrase familiar in the mouths of the superficial members of a jaded society, which is for ever restlessly inventing new fashions, new sensations, new amusements, new excitements, new epigrams, new creeds, new theories; and whose habitual question is, not What is truth? but What is the news? And when we compare the shallow metaphysician of the seventeenth century, to whom the great basal laws of thought appeared trifling propositions, with the poet to whom

> "The meanest flower that blows can give
> Thoughts that do often lie too deep for tears,"

we feel it is only to common minds at common moments that truth of any kind can appear commonplace. I need not apologise, therefore, for obeying the call of Advent Sunday, and preaching upon death. There must come a moment, sooner or later, when the commonplace, "We must all die," will, in the language of our great novelist, transform itself suddenly into the concrete consciousness, "I must die and soon." And I will ask you for a few minutes to forestall that transformation to-night. Picture yourselves, each one of you, lying in his own death-chamber, with the attendants moving softly, and your watch ticking out the minutes, and the food and medicine, now useless, put away from your bedside, and as the shadows close around you, and the walls of your very being seem to fall in upon themselves, and you sink alone into the nothingness, where no human eye can follow you, no human voice can penetrate, no human love can protect you, ask yourselves, my brethren, what it is that will be ending there. Three things will be ending—life, and thought, and love. All the bright physical life of flashing eye, and flushing cheek, and pulsing blood, and its exuberance, and energy, and joy are failing, fainting, fading into pasture for the worm. All the wide range and versatility of intellect, that has so often done more than compensate the loss of bodily capacity by the delirious intoxication of what has seemed to be omnipotence, is narrowing into impotence, imbecility, and nothingness. And last of all, the very love that has shed its lustre over life and thought, and seemed only to gather strength and purity as they successively declined,—love, too, will be passing from you, as you swoon into the darkness, and your nearest and your dearest press their lips to you in vain. Life will have ended, thought will have ended, love will have ended. Aristotle did not exaggerate when he said " Death is of all things the most terrible, for it is the end." Fearfulness and trembling may come upon you, and pain and disappointment add a pang to death; but above and beyond them all it is the ending that is so unutterably sad.

Still, if our span of life were all in sunshine while it lasted, and death came over us like sunset, shadowless and sudden at its close, it might be possible, at least for a season, to keep the thought of it at bay. But it is not so, the inevitable shadow is cast upon us from the cradle, and the fact which we call death is only the last complete expression of a process that has gone on throughout our lives. Look back from your dying chamber over the life of affection that is ending there, and count if you can with how many ruins it is strewed. Friends have died one after another, and you thought at first you could never survive them; but as time went on you found it otherwise; their memory has faded and become ethereal, and at last you can look at their pictures and speak of their names without a pang. Or friends have parted, and for a moment you realised how truly "every parting is an image of death;" but by degrees you cease to write to them, or think of them, or they of you; till at last, in after years, when they are mentioned you say only, Ah! we were great friends *once*, at college, or at school. Think of the burning intensity of schoolboy or college friendship, and then that it should come to this, and ask yourselves, Is not that a real death? And then, even before death, or local separation; jealousy, or reserve, or pride, or difference of taste, of temperament, of opinion, like frost in springtime, has nipped friendship after friendship in the bud. There is not one of you, however young, not one of you however generous, who does not already know, as a fact of personal experience, the death of some affections, foreshadowing the bitter end of all.

It is no otherwise with thought. It may be your fate as you lie dying to be in the possession of all your faculties; but the phrase has little meaning. Think of the vistas of thought which opened out before you when you first woke to the consciousness of intellectual power; remember how you resolved to traverse one after another of them, till you had explored the whole universe of thought; and then how the limitations of your reason were by degrees borne in upon you, and after an interval of restless rebellion you found that you must confine yourself to some one region, and then within that region to some one department, and even there that your originality and memory and comprehension failed you, as the cerebral tissues wasted, till your brain seemed to close in upon you, like the shroud of iron, and at last become the coffin of your thought. To die in the consciousness that your intellectual life has been dying daily—that is what the full possession of your faculties comes to mean.

Meanwhile, what has been the case with the bodily instrument of your thought and affection? What has been the course of your physical life, that has led to such weakness at its close? Put aside the accidental pain and sickness that have helped to kill you, and examine the physical process of living at its best. It might with equal scientific accuracy be described as a process of dying. The same forces, which in combination are the conditions of your life, tend by the very fact of their own persistence to disperse and neutralise themselves. The same process that wore away the life of plants, and the life of animals, and the very fabric of the lands on which they struggled for existence ages upon ages before man began to be, and that is now operant through infinite space, wearing away the energy of suns and stars, and stellar systems, has been wearing away your body from the moment of its birth. We limit the word dissipation, in our moral phraseology, to one or two particular forms of self-destruction. But in scientific language our whole existence is one long dissipation of energy, and it is no exaggeration for a man of science to say "'Debemur morti nos nostraque,' is written over the portals of life." Life is but an episode in an universe of dying.

My brethren, that dying may be converted into a daily sacrifice, offered up to love. First, there is the very exuberance of life's energy and joy. Indulge that to the utmost in the lust of the flesh, and the pride of life, and its speedy end will be decay of the body, decay of the affections, decay of the mind. You need not go to science or religion to assure you of the first, for in exact proportion as you know the sins, you know in yourselves the dread premonitory symptoms, that the end of those things is death, and how at moments they seem to gather half their romance and power of seduction from the subtle indefinable taint of death that clings about them, though it be only for a moment, and only to end in intenser despair. But sacrifice your flesh by discipline, in communion with your Lord, and you will gather daily fresh strength of body, and with it of mind, and of affection, to be converted into fresh channels, and in their turn to be employed, not as instruments of pleasure but of usefulness and work. When the fallacious temptation, "After all, I am only an animal," which has ruined so many souls, comes before you, answer, "Yes, but even animals exist for sacrifice." And when, sooner or later, the flesh grows weak and weary; do not sink, as now-a-days we so often see men sinking, into miserable, selfish valetudinarianism, and make your gathering weakness a plea for taxing others and excusing yourself. No; take your weakness and pain and weariness, as fresh opportunities for sacrifice; if they limit your enjoyments, force them to intensify your love; if they really make work impossible, force them to increase your humility; if they withdraw you from things outward, force them to lead you into the life of prayer; and so, as you mount onward and upward in the ladder of your sacrifice, you will feel at each step that you are conquering Death with his own weapons, that all the deaths of your daily life are being converted into means of life for others; till your end, when it comes, and you can say "It is finished," will only be the completion of your sacrifice, gathering up and flashing out into the lives and hearts of others what has all along been the purpose of your life.

Turn to the intellectual life, and you will find that, too, fraught with the same double possibilities of death and sacrifice. As its range contracts, and its opportunities diminish, and its faculties faint and fail, you can despair of it, and die, or offer it in sacrifice, and make its every death only a moment in the larger life. For example: when you begin to recognise the limitations of your thought, the majority of you are at once tempted to acquiesce in them as final, and to regard the intellectual life as one to which others, but not you, are called. And many of those who would see the fallacy of pleading, It is my nature to live an animal life, are falling victims to the fallacy, It is my nature to be irrational. Every one of you is called to the intellectual life, according to his measure; and it is from the neglect of that call, and the dull acquiescence in the death of Reason, that such an atmosphere of ignorance has spread abroad over the nations, as to make it possible for men to say, and with a show of plausibility, that more evil in the world is due to ignorance than to malice.

If your capacities are small then, do not bury them, wrapped in a napkin, with the cynical epitaph upon their tomb—"Of making many books there is no end, and he that increaseth knowledge increaseth sorrow." Rather accept your limitations and use them in the spirit of sacrifice. Realise that you can never know enough, perhaps, to take a pleasure in the things of thought, but that you can know enough to be of service to your fellows. If, on the other hand, your capacities are comparatively large, remember that they can be only utilised by acceptance of the ascetic principle of the division of labour, which is as necessary in the intellectual as in the social and mechanical world; but far more painful, for it means the abdication of entire realms of thought, and the acceptance of a life of slavery in confinement to one region only, that in the end, instead of honouring you, a younger generation of thinkers may see farther, by means of trampling upon the foundations which you have laid. Use thought as a means to pleasure, and it will crumble at your touch, and you will die murmuring the foolish murmur, There is one end to the wise man and to the fool. Sacrifice it to the help of others, cost the sacrifice what it may, and wisdom will be justified of her children, for they will have learnt that she is a loving spirit.

For the life of thought carries us on once more to the life of love. There are times when we think bodily death and intellectual death endurable, but that, last of all, even love should die is misery indeed. And yet we saw, in our brief review of it, that it is almost the first death which we experience; that there were few of us at this moment who have not, in our measure, felt its agony. My brethren, analyse the death of friendship, and see how it occurs. It occurs because you would possess exclusively what was not meant to be exclusively possessed. You are not content to have your jewel in a cabinet, your picture in a gallery,—you must needs add to the pure pleasure of it the selfish satisfaction of being able to lock it up and say, It is wholly and exclusively mine. And so jealousy creeps in, and jealousy is bitter as the grave. Few, I believe, are fully alive to the enormous moral harm which, in a sensitive emotional atmosphere like that of an Oxford college, has its rise in the subtler forms of jealousy. You revel not in the possession, but in the exclusive possession, of your friend. You are fond of parading to others, by a thousand little touches of phrase or conduct, the fact, or it may be the fiction, that you in reality are the sole object of your friend's affection. And in proportion as you give reason for, you also feel, jealousy, when your friend is taken from you by that God who alone is rightly jealous, because He is conscious of alone possessing the perfect strength, and perfect holiness, and perfect loveliness, and perfect love, which can captivate and satisfy the yearnings of the human heart.

And then, akin to jealousy, is the other cause of the death of friendship, *i.e.* disappointment. You expected your friend to be all-sufficient, quite forgetting that the sufficiency which you are craving, and which alone will satisfy you, is and can be nothing short of infinite. And so, because your friend is not infinite, you break his heart by growing cold to him, and pass on to be embittered by another and another disappointment, and, in the measure of your capacity, to break another and another heart. And so jealousy and disappointment cloud the bright love-light of your youth with darkness, and before half your life is over you are emotionally dead.

Once more then, my brethren, turn round upon and accept the limitations of love, and offer them in sacrifice, and by sacrificing overcome them. Be willing that your friend should love others as much, or more, than you; and make his care for them a reason for including them also in your own affection. Be willing to find limitations, imperfections, weaknesses, in every human soul, and to love them all the more because they are partly to be pitied. And all this will involve a sacrifice, and a sacrifice so real as to be likened in more than metaphor to a gradual daily dying. But it can be offered daily till you are content to give all and ask back nothing; only saying, as friends leave or fall short of your expectations, " The Lord gave and the Lord hath taken away, blessed be the name of the Lord."

Such, my brethren, is sacrifice in life, and thought, and love; and as the death over which it triumphs gathers darkness towards the end, so does the life of sacrifice rise higher as it goes on. It is the familiar mountain-path, of which each peak reveals a higher; but as you climb it, you will gather courage from the keener air, and the widening vision, and the beauty of the flowers that grow nowhere else, till at last the plains and valleys that seemed once so hard to leave lie again stretched out before you, no longer in their isolation, but gathered all into one great harmony in the shadowless light of the full day. And then, but not till then, will you know the meaning of the words, " No man hath left father or mother, or husband or wife, for my sake, but shall receive an hundred-fold in this life, and in the world to come life everlasting."

But you may object, This dying life of sacrifice is very little better than the living death of sin and selfishness. It is an ideal which seems to have suited Stoic philosophers and Indian monks, but it is inadequate to satisfy man, as he stands in despair beside the grave.

My brethren, it would be so if sacrifice belonged only to human life, but, thank God, it is also the law of the Divine. When two human beings are utterly in love with one another, and each yearns to make a sacrifice to the other of his every thought and inclination and whim, till at the last he seems to have emptied himself of his very personality, so far from being annihilated, he is enriched by that very sacrifice, for he receives back the life of the other, with the addition of his own, and each personality is doubled. It is so with the life of sacrifice that, as Christians, you are called to lead. The offering of all your life and thought, and love and energy, is not made to an abstract colourless humanity, but to a Person who is the infinite, eternal, archetypal man. And He in turn has sacrificed life and thought and love to you, that you may receive back the love you gave Him with the addition of that infinite love which is His essence, and all the thought you gave Him made perfect in His infinite wisdom, and the life that you have given up to Him translated into His eternal life of glory.

This, my brethren, is the crown and consummation of the life of sacrifice. But it is also the only means and the pledge of its possibility.

For your Lord does not wait till you are in the grave before he gives Himself to you. He is daily ever offering Himself to you, that you may have strength to persevere in the life of sacrifice to Him ; and if you seek Him there, He will lead you up and on from strength to strength, and over heights of sacrifice before undreamed of, till, from the mountain-summit of your deathbed all the shadows fall away as you pass upward into union with the Three Persons of that Holy Trinity, whose perfect sacrifice of each to other makes Them absolutely One.

II.

TROUBLE.

"It is good for me that I have been in trouble; that I might learn Thy statutes."—Ps. cxix. 71.

TIMES of political decadence are times of spiritual growth. For the very fact that men see the institutions and traditions of their childhood, and the prospects of their friends and families, and the future of their country, inevitably doomed, forces them to take shelter in the spiritual region, from the storm that is sweeping outward things away. And so it is out of the inner experience of hidden lives, in ages when statesmen saw little hope, that such priceless contributions have been made to the devotional treasury of humanity, as the hymn of Cleanthes—the meditations of Aurelius—the Confessions of Augustine—the Imitation of

Christ. But first and foremost among these products of the ages of the hidden life is the great psalm of which my text is the summary—" It is good for me that I have been in trouble; that I might learn Thy statutes." To the literary critic it has all the notes of a silver age. Its structure is artificial, its language stereotyped, its length excessive, its thought monotonous. It must be almost the latest utterance of the dying voice of Hebrew psalmody. And yet the words of this nameless sufferer epitomise exhaustively the religious aspirations and joys and sorrows of the human soul, and have remained —and will remain, without a doubt, to the end of time—the great manual of Christian devotion.

And at a time like the present, when national calamities abroad, and startling catastrophes at home, have been forcing upon all thoughtful men the problem of the sorrow of the world, it would be well to strengthen our wavering faith by looking as boldly as did the Psalmist, at the spiritual fruitfulness of sorrow; and to ask ourselves whether we are making our own sorrows bear their fruit.

The earliest form of trouble is for most of us physical pain, and our instinctive tendency is to view pain as an unmitigated evil. We try to forget it in youth, and to minimise it in age, and, now-a-days, even dally with systems of opinion which advocate its termination by a narcotic euthanasia. But, after all, such a view of pain is not in accordance with the facts of life. For, not to mention its many other and more mysterious aspects, pain is beyond question the great educator of the soul. Without it we should slumber on, and in proportion as they are without it, men do slumber, prolonging childhood into youth, and youthfulness into maturity, till they wake with a start to find life over, and its lessons unlearned, and its work undone. But pain counteracts all this. Pain pierces in a moment the frail fabric of the dreams of sense—and flashes lightning through and through their unsubstantial, unenduring emptiness — rousing men to ask themselves where permanence and rest are to be found— that rest which is, after all, the deepest craving of the human soul,—and forcing them sooner or later, whether they will or no, back upon the recognition of that spiritual reality, of which sense, and its life, and its pleasure, are partial and limited expressions, and in virtue of that limitation destined of necessity to pass away. In a word, pain makes men real. It indurates their character. It endows them with spiritual insight. It initiates them into the meaning and inner truth of things. Greek prophecy, no less than Hebrew, foresaw, by the light of nature, that the utterly real man must be a man of sorrows and acquainted with grief. But, beyond all this, by investing a man with a greater amount of reality—pain invests him with a mysterious attractiveness for others—as a material body attracts others in precise proportion to its bulk. First, we are drawn to sympathise with a fellow-creature in his suffering, but as we contrast our two conditions, sympathy passes into awe. There is a heroism in the very fact of suffering which lifts the sufferer above us, and makes us feel that he is moving in a realm of being to us unknown, till our sympathy is hushed into something of awestruck admiration, and from the blending of sympathy with awe comes love. This is the secret which has made so many a bed of helpless, hopeless suffering, the centre from which others have derived all their help and hope, and has invested, age after age, those who have been called to follow the Man of Sorrows, with a shadow of that great prerogative which enabled Him to say " I, if I be lifted up from the earth, will draw all men unto me."

But pain is, after all, but the beginning of troubles. ,We can bear to see a friend in pain when we know that he will rise from it the stronger ; and we can bear to undergo pain, in our turn, when we know that it is but drawing closer the links and bonds of sympathy and affection that surround us. But there is the pain which does not unite, but separates—the pain which ends in death ; death that year by year removes more of our friends and companions, till it has cast its shadow at last on our every " good-night " and " good-bye." Look below the surface, and death is everywhere. Society is another name for dissociation.

Differences of character and age and occupation, and all the artificial necessities of our complex civilisation, are for ever at work to break up families, and separate friends, and estrange acquaintance, till the progress of life becomes another name for a journey into the wilderness, there to die alone. But if it is good for us to have been in the trouble of pain, still more is it good for us to have been in the trouble of parting. For, if ever our Master could say of His earthly presence, "It is expedient for you that I go away," much more must this be true of every lesser human parting. As long as we cling to the visible presence of our friends, as all in all, we are clinging to a shadow that will fade from us with the setting of the sun. Then comes the awful blank of parting, to open our eyes, and teach us the true conditions of every real human friendship, as having only its point of departure in the outward and visible region, but its goal in that spiritual communion which outward accidents cannot affect, but which is only possible through union with Him, in whom all spirits have their being. And so the use of death and parting is not to end our human ties, but to translate them into that region where alone they can be everlasting. Nor does this trouble, any more than other trouble, end with its effect on self. The man whom God has widowed of the visible presences of earthly friends, is not only the stronger man. He is also the more influential. There is a fascination about the solitary character which cannot help making itself felt, even when the solitude is self-elected and misanthropic. Far greater, therefore, is the fascination exercised by those who have learned, by the sad removal of one tie after another, to centre their affections in the spiritual region, and by so doing, to invest them with the universality of the spirit, and to love no longer a few only, but the world. These are those barren ones who have more children than they which have an husband—and who, because they have left house or brethren, or sisters, or father, or mother, or wife, shall receive an hundred-fold now in this time, houses and brethren, and sisters, and mothers, and children, and lands—with persecutions.

But there is yet another trouble which casts a shadow upon death itself—the trouble of doubt. We can bear to part with our loved ones as long as the outlines of that spiritual country to which we know that they are tending, stand out clear on the sunset horizon. But when the clouds have come down on the mountains, and we send them out into the midnight storm, seeing and knowing nothing of their path, or of its goal, then death and parting take a darker hue. And many men who are willing enough to believe other troubles to be good and God-sent, shrink back cowardly from the pain of doubt, as if that alone were devil-born. But it is not so. From the moment when the cry, "My God, my God, why hast Thou forsaken me?" went up out of the deep of the midday midnight upon Calvary, doubt was for ever consecrated as the last trial of the sons of God—and a trial needed for their purification, no less than pain or parting. For consider what it is that doubt effects for us. From the moment when we first grow conscious of spiritual truth in childhood, we invest it with the shape and colouring which our teachers or circumstance suggest, and these pictures which our imagination draws, as a setting and framework for the truth, are like the pleasures of sense, or the presence of friends —the first manifestations of spiritual life. But, as in the two former cases, they are not the life itself. For the truth of God is infinite— ever-young, ever-growing, ever-new; while the forms in which imagination clothes it are finite, and borrowed from the past. And we are forced therefore, in proportion as our hold upon truth is fast and firm, to be for ever finding the old formulæ too straitened to express it— the old bottles unfitted for containing the new wine. The belief of our fathers, expressed as they expressed it, must, by the very fact that it was real to them, have for us a touch of unreality. And there comes the pain of doubt. A thousand tender associations, and holy memories, and glorious hopes, are so intimately inwoven in the tissue that clothes our creed, that truth in a new garment seems at first to be no truth at all, or at least to be an unpractical, abstract, barren, lifeless thing. We are being led of the Spirit into the wilderness, and we think our faith is gone. But the real nature of the change which your faith is being called to undergo is only the change of health when pain comes, or of friendship in the hour of parting. It is only the cutting away of all that is relative, to bring out the eternal sculpture; the bursting through its sheath, by the quickened force of the expanding bud. It is the acquisition of a new, a personal, a spiritual grasp of truth, which thenceforward nothing accidental or external can unloose. But it is more than this. It is also the resetting of the picture, the refacing of the gem. For divine truth is not a science that is already complete and classified. It is for ever alive, and awaits development at the hands of each succeeding age. For men are separate personalities, each endowed with some individual character, some peculiar difference from all the world beside. Each of you is a new species in the spiritual universe, and your mission is not only to appropriate, but also to transform the truth, to exhibit a new aspect, to reflect a new ray, and so to transmit it to others with a new, a superadded glory—the glory that it has received in the act of your acceptance and your transmission. And your reward is like your mission, peculiar to yourself. For it is the reception of that "new name written, which no man knoweth save he that receiveth it." And all your dissatisfaction, all your impatience with bygone phrases, all your throes, and agonies and travail-pangs of doubt, are part of the night-long wrestling, through which that new name is to be won.

Doubt, then, like pain and death, is a messenger of blessing, not only to its sufferer, but through him to other men. And, however much we speculate upon the cause of this mysterious law, the fact remains that here and now, in the world of our experience, it is good for us to have been in trouble. And if this be so, we ought boldly to utilise our troubles as they come. It is too much the custom to think it manly, if not positively virtuous, to ignore the lighter afflictions of life, and leave the lesson of sorrow to be learned only from the sadder experience of overwhelming woe. Instead of this, you should go forward to meet your sorrows, not multiplying them by false asceticism, but looking them in the face when they come upon you, and resolving that as you go through the vale of misery you *will* use it for a well. Do not think any sorrow too trivial to be charged with spiritual meaning, and turn an ear to the divine message because it is lisped by the mouths of infant angels. For it is out of the mouths of such babes and sucklings that God has ordained strength. Unless you learn the use of minor sorrows, the greater ones will only drive you into cynicism or despair. But if you have early learned its meaning, then its each successive appearance will no longer seem other than the arrival of a friend.

It is natural, at first, to feel such an attitude unmanly, for we so instinctively regard action, achievement, conquest of some form or other, as our ideal for humanity, that it requires an effort to accustom the mind to what seems, at first sight, the very converse view. But make the effort. Place yourselves for a moment beyond the pressure of present prejudice, and look back upon the past. Whom, as a matter of fact, do you regard as the greatest heroes of past history, but the men whose great achievements have been wrought out through suffering? And whom do you recognise, whom does the most active antichristian opinion of necessity consent to recognise, as at least the highest human hero, but Him whose life was one long suffering, and whose greatest action was His Passion?

Yes, brethren, in the face merely of the human history of Jesus Christ, and of all who have in any way followed Him along His way of sorrows, you cannot but feel that suffering is not only the road to supreme achievement, but is in itself the highest heroism,—the heroism in which the human most nearly touches the Divine.

But to the Christian it is more than this. It is also the point in which the Divine has touched the human, and by that touch removed the last barrier between the spirit of man and the acceptance of sorrow. For, when all has been said that can be said of the human side of sorrow, there still remain the importunate questions with which man turns upon his Maker: Why was sorrow needed? Why hast Thou made me thus? And to that question the Incarnation gives the one sufficient answer— "Come and see." Speculative satisfaction He has not given, and, in a sense, He could not give us. But by suffering for and with us He appeals to our love to follow Him, and so to learn — in the one only way, the way of personal experience—how, at least in this our present state, sorrow is a needful part of sacrifice, and sacrifice is love in action, and God is love.

"These are they which came out of great tribulation, and have washed their robes, and made them white in the blood of the Lamb. *Therefore* are they before the throne of God, and serve Him day and night in His temple: and He that sitteth on the throne shall dwell among them."

III.

ETERNITY.

"The things which are seen are temporal; but the things which are not seen are eternal."—2 COR. iv. 18.

BRETHREN, there is an advantage in being called on twice to contemplate the beginning and the ending of the year. For the beginning and the ending, though they can only exist together, can, by us whose thoughts are serial, only be realised apart. And so it is well that we are called in Advent to think of the close of life and time, leaving new hopes and new resolves and new beginnings for the opening of the secular year. Then something of the bitterness of death is past and over, and we can feel the first faint tinglings of the spring in our veins, turning the shadow of our death into the morning. But now "change and decay" are everywhere around us—leaves falling, cold gathering, days darkening—desolation, nakedness, winter, death. And despair forces us, as it forced our ancestors in long pre-Christian ages, to prophesy that death and darkness are not, cannot be, the end. And Christianity takes up and transforms the heart's vague prophecy into sure prediction, by reminding us of that eternity which underlies all change.

It is therefore of eternity that nature and the Church alike are calling you to think. And now, if ever, there is need of our rendering obedience to the call. For, apart from all sentimental depreciation of the age we live in, it is an age of distractions, and we glory in the fact. Patriarchal meditation in the fields at the eventide; oriental watchfulness among the midnight stars; Greek philosophy, thought out when schools were still the homes of leisure; monastic detachment; renaissance learning; even the stately literature of the last century; are now impossible to us, for repose has utterly perished from our lives; and we think hastily, and read superficially, and speak and write and act prematurely, and possibly save time, but certainly lose eternity. "Unto whom I sware in my wrath that they should not enter into my rest."

I will ask you, therefore, to meditate upon the eternity of unseen things as a present fact, which gives its reality to all your fair life of nature now, and now and not in a dim future, crowns its death with glory. To realise this, I know, requires an effort; for we have heard the far-off music of the word "eternity" so often, that it has ceased to have much meaning for our ears; and we are content to think of it vaguely as something that will come after "time," and then turn out to be only "time" of a more monotonous description. And so when Holy Scripture speaks of eternal life, and eternal fire, and inhabiting eternity, and the eternal city, and the unseen things which are eternal, the impression left upon our minds is of everlasting counterparts of the things we see around us, an endless repetition of the wear and tear of time.

To some extent, I know, we cannot help this mode of thinking, because it is the very law and condition of all our thought that we should express spiritual and supersensual ideas, like "GOD" and "soul" and "immortality," by words which involve a metaphor borrowed from the things of sense. But this law is no fatality to be accepted in passive acquiescence; for however much it may curb and limit and make ridiculous our pride of intellect, it stimulates, and was meant to stimulate, our intellectual sloth. The very fact that at the best we can know so little of the great realities is a reason for our pressing onward, grappling with them, wrestling with them, refusing with passionate insistance to let them go till we know their name.

Eternity then is rather the quality of timelessness, than a quantity of time. It is out of, and above, and beneath, and behind time. It does not go on for ever, but it always is; and to introduce into it the temporal notions of after and before, is like attempting to cut water with an axe. It is measured by its intensity, not by its extension. And because timeless, things eternal are whole, and self-identical and changeless—" the same yesterday, to-day, and for ever."

Brethren, perhaps you may think this a needlessly metaphysical conception—a fossil from some intellectual stratum of bygone ages, which will hardly repay the labour of its disinterment in these busy days.

But I assure you it is not so. Notions, like eternity, can only be made real to us by accumulating epithets, and then recognising that all together are inadequate, much more refusing to be content with any one. And the indolent acquiescence in the use of the word everlasting, as the stereotyped translation of the fulness of the thought "eternal," has weakened our hold on the present reality of the unseen things which are eternal, till some forget them, and others doubt them, and others again deny that they exist; and yet, if you will only face and interrogate your own minds and hearts and wills, you will find the evidence for eternity too persistent to be soon forgotten, too obvious to be doubted of, too importunate to be denied.

First ask your minds why the great truths of

thought are so unchanging. Why are the fundamental axioms of logic, or of mathematics, no older now than they were in the days of Aristotle and of Euclid? Why are the precepts of the moral law, "Thou shalt love . . . ." and "Thou shalt not covet . . . ." no older now than for Confucius, or for Buddha, or for Moses? How can they have retained their sameness through all the change of ages, and have not been touched by time? Simply because they are eternal, and therefore always self-identical, independent of the brains that think them, independent of the lapse of time.

Or again, take human emotion. When you read, and read, and realise words such as "Jacob served seven years for Rachel; and they seemed unto him but a few days, for the love he had to her;" or when you listen to the story of those two friends in the Reign of Terror, who parted on the scaffold with the words, "Our heads will meet in the sack," and your heart rises in rebellious consciousness that their love was truer than their creed; or when in some great crisis you had lived a lifetime in an instant, or in the rare moments of supreme devotion fathomed the depths of joy or sorrow ;—do you not know, and with a certitude beyond need of further evidence, that you live and breathe in the atmosphere of a world which is eternal—eternal and beyond the touch of time?

Or again, if you are not emotional, perhaps you have strong wills. Consider then your will, and as it resolves, executes, repents, controls thought, guides emotion, changes the future, and undoes the past, you must be conscious that in its every action you are traversing the laws of time. In virtue of your wills you claim to be at liberty, independent, free; and nothing in time is at liberty, nothing in time is independent, nothing in time is free. Absolute dependence is the condition of all things temporal; and the very words therefore that you have stereotyped in your everyday language are a witness that your wills belong to eternity and not to time.

And behind all these partial faculties is the personality, the self within you, of which thought, and emotion, and will are the external manifestations. That too is eternal. And thence it is that the scenes which we lived in long ago, the pleasures that we once enjoyed, the pains that are passed and over, come back to us pale and ghostlike—for they have died the death of time; while our thoughts, and words, and actions, of evil or of good—the first lie, the first wrong thought, the first anger with a brother, or the first little act of charity, or heroism, or self-denial—are as real now to us as they ever were, because they are a part, a real part, of our unseen personality, and "the things which are not seen are eternal." You have no need then to go further in quest of evidence about eternity; for the testimony of your own consciousness—the most infallible of witnesses, the witness that you can live by, and the witness that you must die by—assures you that your own inmost personalities are eternal, and that the three essential faculties through which your personalities radiate—your thoughts, your affections, and your wills—are but so many avenues of access to that unseen world which is eternal.

But, brethren, if all this be so, there is surely a fatal fallacy in contrasting the present life with that of the world which is to come, as if the one were wholly temporal, and the other alone eternal; as if here and now, at any rate, we could be satisfied with the things of time, and only resigned them because we could never carry them away with us beyond the grave.

Here and now, in the mysterious depths of your inner being, you are eternal; and in reality there are not, there never were, two courses open to you. Eternal life is the necessity of your nature, and if you try to have it otherwise, your every faculty is witness against you, as with gathering impatience it casts aside one after another of the things of time, till you wake to recognise here and now that by your rejection of life eternal you have only gained its opposite —not life temporal, but eternal death.

Again, I will ask you to appeal to the evidence of all history, and of your own experience, that this is a fact. For, take the possible objects of thought—art, and science, and philosophy. Again and again in the course of history, in ancient Greece, in mediæval Italy, closer still, in modern Oxford, men have tried to find intellectual satisfaction in the world of art, and have not found it. They think, and it is gone, the beautiful world of art—melted like the statue Michael Angelo carved in snow. And why? Because thought demands in things fixity, permanence, finality. Without these it cannot be satisfied; and they are not to be found in art.

And so men turn to science for intellectual satisfaction; but intellectual satisfaction is not to be found in science. Add science to science till you have traced the past history of the whole great universe, from the luminous cloud which once it was, or may have been, through all the successive stages of its miraculous development, and explored the secrets of all the motion · and life and thought with which it teems, and prophesied the distant day when all its forces shall be worn out again, and motion and life and thought shall be no more; but still your reason will be dissatisfied, and ask, Why was it all thus? Why did universal history take this course and not another? Show me not only that it was so, but that it could not have been otherwise. And science cannot answer you. Its results are empirical, contingent, probable. It cannot satisfy the postulates of reason. It is at best a grand *perhaps*.

And so men make one more effort, and pass from science to philosophy. Philosophy sums up the intellectual region, and if there is no speculative satisfaction in philosophy, there is certainly none anywhere at all. But, brethren, the failure of human philosophy is a commonplace. Those who know nothing else of her, know at least that she has failed—failed to answer in the last resort that importunate question, "Why?" failed to show that necessity for things being as they are, which is the constant, uncompromising, inexorable demand of reason.

Art and science and philosophy then have altogether failed to provide us as rational beings with intellectual satisfaction, because their results are partial, and therefore perishable and changing, while reason demands to know things in their wholeness, their unity, their permanence; in a word, under their eternal form. It is still the contrast, as of old: "They shall wax old as doth a garment;" " but Thou art the same, and Thy years shall not fail."

If any of you have failed to follow my meaning here, you will find the same fact still clearer on looking at the emotional side of your nature. Do the human affections find adequate satisfaction among the things of time? The first object presented to them is the family and the family life; and what is the common history of English families in the present day? Difference of age, idiosyncrasy of temperament, diversity of pursuit, little by little part one from another, and resolve the family back again into its component atoms. And even where this is not the case, does the most ideal family, can it ever, fully satisfy the infinite cravings of the human heart? The experience of every one of you will immediately answer "No," or you would not be impelled, as you are impelled, to seek for further objects of interest in self-chosen friendship and self-chosen love.

But are these in their turn adequate, as long as their source is in the region of time? Look back upon the history of your friendships from childhood till now. One has been added to another with increasing fever of intensity. And each, when first you formed it, promised to be infinite and adequate; and yet each has been touched with something of sadness in the end. You had hoped it would be all in all to you, and discover some depth which it cannot reach; and, disappointed and disillusioned, you cry to the Eternal in your loneliness, " There is none upon earth that I desire in comparison of Thee." And hereafter you will find it the same in the third great relation of human affection. That too will turn out inadequate, if it is founded on the things of time.

There is one other region, as we have seen, in which our personality is manifested. It is the region of the will. You have all heard of the tears of Alexander, weeping for worlds to conquer; but Alexander was neither the first nor the last to weep such tears. Conquest, material conquest, is the most obvious mode and symbol of the self-assertion of the human will; and you may read therefore in the history of conquest the entire history of the human will, for ever claiming nothing less than its own absolute supremacy, and never attaining to more than a relative success: "To will is present with me ... but how to perform I know not." And so the human will, like human thought and human affection, is driven home to the Eternal, and says, "I will not let thee go."

To whatever region then we turn for evidence the answer is the same. No temporal object of thought, no temporal object of affection, no temporal object of will ever has, or ever can, provide an adequate satisfaction for the cravings of our unseen, eternal personality. This is not a truth to be received in faith, despite of evidence to the contrary. There is no evidence to the contrary; all the evidence points one way. It is a fact, a plain, palpable, inevitable fact, as familiar as the experience of our everyday lives, if only we would open our eyes to see, and our ears to hear it. Eternity exists. We are eternal, and our true life also is by consequence eternal.

Brethren, there is an old doctrine, much in vogue among modern thinkers, which ascribes the sin and sorrow of the world to ignorance, to men not knowing what belongs unto their peace. If only you will face these facts with honesty, and realise in the quiet of thought what are the conditions of your true existence, you will find it easier, because more reasonable, to turn yourselves and all your faculties to Him in the knowledge of Whom standeth your eternal life. In His light you will read truly the meaning of the things of time ; of temporal knowledge in the light of the Eternal Wisdom ; of temporal affection in the light of the Eternal Love ; of temporal will in the light of the Eternal Power ; of all together, when they are focused in a human personality, in the light of the three Eternals Which are one Eternal. And then, instead of being dissatisfied with their obvious limitations, you will love them the more—the dying nature, and the unsatisfying thought, and the inadequate affection, and the helpless, heart-broken will—for proclaiming by the very fact of their imperfection that they are not that Light, but are sent out to bear witness of that Light. For that Light is the life of men, the eternal life that shall endure, when the angel shall have sworn by Him that liveth for ever and ever that time shall be no longer.

IV.

THE CONSEQUENCES OF SIN.

"The wrath of the Lamb."—REV. vi. 16.

THERE is always a great danger in spiritual reactions, for reactions involve the oblivion of one aspect of truth or another, and this mutilation of their harmony is fatal to the things of the spirit. It is especially so at the present day with the doctrine of the punishment of sin. There has been a widespread and a needful reaction amongst us, against the crudity of the logic, and the grotesqueness of the imagination, which conspired to curse the world with the mediæval conception of hell; *but* in their eagerness to be quit of an unpleasant bugbear, men seem to be forgetting that underneath that mediæval conception, with all its coarse materialism, there breathed the intense conviction of more spiritual minds than ours, that sin was a terrible reality, fraught with terrible results; and it would be well for a generation, that has long ceased to look at nature in the light of the Bible, at least to be true to its own principles of observation and experiment, and look honestly at the Bible in the light thrown on it by the indisputable facts of nature. Now, there is no point upon which modern science has insisted with greater emphasis than on the slightness of the causes needed to produce infinitely great results. The sculpture of the mountains, the upheaval of the continents, the deep engraving of the lines that sever the races of animals and men, are the result of causes which, if we could see them at any one moment of their operation, are absolutely infinitesimal, and bring home to us with a new meaning the old philosophic warning, "Despise not thou the day of small things."

But it is the darker aspect of this truth that I would ask you now to contemplate, the awful power of nature's forces, when we thwart them, to destroy us, the terribly impartial severity of the least of nature's laws. There is no fairer thing of beauty than a mountain glistening between heaven and earth, in all the glory of a summer sunrise. But one false step in ascending it, and the laws of gravitation know no mercy. The bright symbol of glory, and purity, and heavenly aspiration, is changed into an awful minister of death ; and men look up at it with trembling, as to the great headstone of a sepulchre. For centuries there was no more perfect type of down-trodden submissiveness than that presented by the peasantry of France ; till, in a twinkling, the storm of their anger burst upon astonished Europe, and the flower of chivalry learnt to realise, as they withered in its lightnings, that the patient abiding of the meek could not perish for ever. It is the same in the social as in the physical world. We are proud of the successive triumphs by which human ingenuity has bent the great cosmic forces one after another to its will, and fashioned the once discordant elements of savagery and barbarism into free and enlightened upholders of civilised society. But in both cases nature has only after all been conquered by obeying her, and the penalty of disobedience seems ironically out of proportion to the fault. A flaw in the metal of our machinery, for which no one seems responsible, will in a moment convert the sea from a highroad into a grave; the sleep of a tired official, too long on his post, will condemn a hundred helpless travellers to torture or to death. The selfishness of a single statesman may plunge nations into war.; and an epigram has before now lighted the fires of revolution. Everywhere the same stern law operates, and infinitesimal transgressions produce infinite results.

We might naturally expect, therefore, when we turn to the more delicate machinery and more complex activities of the moral and spiritual life, to find still more serious disorders consequent on the slightest breach of law. And so it is. Take, for example, the sins of the flesh—and consider for a moment the softness of their beginning and the hardness of their end—the joy, the gaiety, the romantic halo that cluster round them and disguise their nature, whispering softly, "Ye shall be as gods, ye shall not surely die;" and then the subtle progress of gradual degradation, as the health is wasted, and the strength enfeebled, and the reason darkened, and the conscience dulled; one grace after another fading, one power after another failing, till the vice alone is left remaining in hideous unabashed relief, and its miserable victims creep away to die in solitude, execrated, outcast, helpless, hopeless, the body crumbling into ruin, and the soul into despair. "She saith to him, Stolen waters are sweet, and bread eaten in secret is pleasant. But he knoweth not that the dead are there; and that her guests are in the depths of hell."

Or, again, take the sin of intemperance—its easy attraction and its awful end. Wine that is so pleasant, wine that is so beautiful—repairing strength, increasing power, facilitating speech, calming sorrow, making merry the heart of man, used by all nations, praised in all ages, consecrated alike by our Master to social joy and solemn memory—is even more insidious in its evil influence than lust. For its use has no uniform limit, its abuse no uniform beginning. Its fascination steals over a man almost unawares. And yet when we hear the words, "at the last it biteth like a serpent and stingeth like an adder," we feel that they are all too pale to express the irreparable ruin that it works.

Once more, take a spiritual sin, and consider the history of pride. We speak of a "proper pride" as an essential element in character, without which one would fall below the dignity of man: we even say that a man *ought* to take a pride in his work, or appearance, or attainments, as if it gave backbone to the life. And yet pride slowly isolates a man from his fellows, his friends, his family. It leads him on to affect virtues, or capacities, or wealth, or rank, or strength, which he does not in fact possess. It is a lying spirit, beguiling him on to a life of ever-increasing hollowness, till at last his only refuge from exposure is in death. The suicide of the fraudulent speculator, the discovered adulterer, the discredited parent or teacher, is a twice-told tale; but be sure that a mind must be far gone in sorrow before it can come to that.

Brethren, you may say these are no fair pictures of average humanity. At any rate they are far more frequent than you perhaps imagine, and our neglect of their terrible warning is due mainly to the fact that we see only their bright beginnings, in the fulness of the daylight; while, as the shadow comes upon them, they creep away into the holes and corners, and another generation take their place in our sight. The top of the wave may always be seen sparkling in the sunshine, and we forget that every moment its particles are changing, and passing, almost before we can look upon them, into the darkness of the abyss. *But*, even granting that these are to be considered exceptional cases, is the picture of average humanity a brighter one to look upon—the picture, that is, of the man who has carried no sin to its excessive consequence, but led simply a self-centred life? Look at him, in youth, as he may be among you now, full of health, and strength, and beauty, and hope, and high ideals, and reach of intellect, and warmth of love; and then look at him in his old age—γῆρας ἄμορφον, as the Greeks called it, with a shudder. The course of the life-blood is a labour and a pain, and the rippling muscles have collapsed into shrivelled imbecility, and the beauty sunk into hollow shapelessness, visibly prophetic of its nearly-approaching ruin in the tomb; while the dull mind that glimmers feebly through the faded eyes has given up all hope, and seen through all ideals, and knows that intellect is nothingness, and love is a delusion, and wastes the short breath that is left him, under pretence of imparting his experience, in trying to make others prematurely like himself. The sensualist and the suicide were at least to be pitied in their end—but the death of the average man of the world is only and utterly contemptible.

This is no exaggeration of the visible consequences of individual sins in individual lives. But this is only the beginning of the picture of moral evil; for the wages of sin are paid with a fearful compound interest, and the real terror of evil is that it does not die with its immediate author. It lives with a strange vicarious life, ramifying, developing, multiplying, hideously replenishing the earth,—till the lust of one ancestor, and the intemperance of another, and the pride and the jealousy and the selfishness of others, have intertwined and interwoven and invested their posterity with a thousand incapacities, and hindrances, and weaknesses, and tendencies to evil,—and the world has become one great discord of pain, and sorrow, and misunderstanding, and intellectual failure, and moral palsy, and spiritual death.

It is a simple fact then, of everyday experience, that moral evil works a ruin to the individual and to the race, of which the "quenchless fire" and the "undying worm" are no inappropriate description; and, apart from any theory as to the nature and origin of evil, or of its fate in the after world, there is enough of terror in its present effects upon the innocent as well as the guilty to insure the loathing of all true-hearted men; and if we could only come to realise more vividly "the pity of it," "the pity of it"—the unutterable piteousness of that terrible entail of woe that our sins bequeath to tender women and innocent children, and the thousands of patient, toiling, broken-hearted poor, there would be less impurity, less sloth, less pride, to desolate the world.

But when all this has been said, there still remains the fact that man feels and knows himself to be a spiritual being, compelled by his very nature to look before and after, to pierce behind the veil of sense to the deep realities which it conceals, to wrestle and grapple with all great problems, and force them to give an account of themselves, to hasten from facts to their causes, from the question " what ?" to the question " why ?"

And so, throughout the ages, man has been incessantly impelled to ask—What there is in moral evil more than meets the eye ? What sin will turn out to be when we see it in the light of the real world ? And if we still confine ourselves to observation of history, quite apart from revelation, Shakespeare's words are literally true —" The weariest and most loathed worldly life that age, ache, penury, and imprisonment can lay on nature, is a paradise to what we fear of death."

The judgment of man upon himself—whether we gather it from savage races, or from the remote beliefs of Egypt, or of our own Indo-European ancestors, or from the truest-sighted intellect of intellectual Greece—has been, that the consequences of sin *cannot* but last beyond the grave. "Where is Ardiœus the Great?" asks the spirit in Plato's vision, and is answered, "He shall not come forth from hell for ever."

Nor can it be maintained for a moment by any serious critic that this universal judgment of man upon himself is due to the invention of an interested priestcraft. It is simply the expressed conviction of the human conscience in all ages that moral evil is a thing infinitely greater and more terrible than even those terrible results of it which we see in this present world; and though we now revolt from the mediæval thoughts of an arbitrary punishment, it is not so easy to escape the suspicion that, amid the universal reign of law, there may be such things as "inevitable consequences," and a wrong step amid the great machinery, hurry us we know not where.

Brethren, if you will from time to time think upon these facts—the *fact* of the present consequences of moral evil, and the *fact* of the gloomy forebodings with which the sight of those consequences, time out of mind, has filled the heart of man—you will be in less danger of the popular modern fallacy, which insults alike both the human dignity and the divine, by promising to sin, apart from repentance, an amiable obliteration, and forgetting that hell, after all, may be the last prerogative of the human will.

V

LIFE.

"I am the Life."—S. JOHN xiv. 16.

LIFE, and the date and the nature of its origin, and the conditions of its maintenance, and the causes of its decay, are subjects with which we are daily growing more and more familiar. Science has traced life back into ages where its presence was once undreamed of, and down into forms of matter, once called inanimate and dead, and on into a future of indefinite, infinite progression, and can modify it, and prolong it, and almost create it; and yet Science cannot tell us what life is. It is defined for us in a hundred ways, by its causes, or its conditions, or its consequences; but causes and conditions and consequences after all are not the life, any more than a man's parentage and circumstances and epitaph are the living human-hearted man.

There is especial need therefore in the present day, that we call to our minds from time to time that other aspect of the mystery of life which Science can illuminate, but could never have revealed; and in the light of that Book, which we know so well was never meant to teach us science, but which does teach us, and was meant to teach us, the philosophy of science, the ultimate first principles on which all science must depend, consider the Word, the Co-eternal, Personal Word of GOD, as not only the Creator, but the present Controller and Sustainer of all possible modes of life.

We are too apt to isolate the Incarnation from its place and context in theology, in history, in nature, and by so doing to mutilate our notions of them all. But, rightly viewed, the Incarnation is but the climax, and fulfilment, and inevitable consequence of the first act of creation; for, as says a modern theologian, quoting the mind of S. Athanasius, "that first act of creation could not stand alone; other acts necessarily followed. Creation and conservation must go together. The finite could not stand of itself; nay, the finite could not have borne the direct action of the infinite upon it, as it started into existence under the divine hand, unless by the infinite itself it had been fortified to bear its touch; otherwise it would fall back into its original nothing, destroyed by the very process of creation. In order then to give effect to His work, He Who was at the first instant external to it must without a moment's delay enter into it, and give it a supernatural strength by His as it were connatural presence," becoming the first-born of His own creation.

It is for this reason that Christian philosophy can see more than poetic fiction in the early creeds that peopled the world with personalities and powers, full of mysterious sympathy and kinship with the joys and sorrows of the sons of men—more than a logical abstraction in that yearning, wistful Pantheism to which men clung amid the miserable dying-days of Greece and Rome—more than mere materialism in the faith of modern science, discerning in matter the promise and potency of all terrestrial life— more even than he was aware of in the language of the psalmist: "He maketh the winds His messengers, and the flames of fire his ministers;" "Fire and hail, snow and vapours, wind and storm fulfilling His Word."

Brethren, I will ask you to trace this presence for a moment through the gradual evolution of the world.

First and lowest, as we call it, in the scale of being, there is matter, and matter is alive— with a strange, unfathomable life of its own. The life of matter is force. Force first gathered it up into systems of sun and star; and force has, through infinite ages, controlled and guided its every movement; from the rush of the comets, and the poising of the planets, and the lightning, and the earthquake, to the lapse of a river, the flight of an insect, the flicker of a sunbeam, the fall of a leaf. But force has another aspect. It is not only present in the activity of nature, it is present also in her rest. And the seeming quiet of the sky, the rock, the lake, the woods, the pasture-land, is quick, to the eye of science, with ceaseless, countless modes of energy; while their every component atom is held in place by the play of forces.

Force then, in rest or motion, is literally everywhere. It persists; it is irresistible; to all appearance it is eternal. And what is force? It is, in its twofold aspect of gentleness and terror, of peace in activity and activity in peace, the first and simplest phase of the communicated energy of Him Who is the Life.

There is a grave in an Alpine village of one who died upon the Riffelhorn, and it is marked with the inscription: "It is I, be not afraid." Brethren, that is the Christian attitude towards the forces of the natural world.

But force, with all its intensity, is only the beginning of life. Gradually, imperceptibly, we pass up to the trees and the flowers, and find ourselves in the presence of a new development of being. The old force, which is the life of matter, still underlies and sustains and informs it, but clothed upon, enriched, transfigured, glorified with fresh capacities. It has entered on a higher life—the life of expansiveness and growth. Force was as impatient of increase as it was of diminution; but the new life of the flower and the forest can increase, and multiply, and replenish the earth. "The grain of mustard-seed, when it is sown in the earth, is less than all the seeds that be in the earth: but when it is sown, it groweth up, and shooteth out great branches; so that the fowls of the air may lodge under the shadow of it."

Yes, the fowls of the air are to lodge under the shadow of it; for the plant-world in turn issues in a life higher than its own—endued with all its forcefulness, its beauty, its expansiveness, but with the new, the superadded capability of feeling. Life is now not only lived; it is also loved.

And yet as the light grows, so does the darkness. As the life of force had its silent intervals, so has the life of growth, and the life of sensibility. The same geologic record that tells of life, tells of death also; and death is not a solitary episode in life; it is inwoven into its

F

very texture by the perpetual recurrence of night-time, and of winter, and of sleep, and of pain. And so if the mystery of force was great, the mysteries of growth and sensibility, with their attendant shadows, are still greater. We cannot draw lines of distinction between their respective provinces, or tell at what stage in the process each new faculty began to be, or what is the real nature of the change we call decay. And even if by accurate attention to due conditions we could actually produce life from out of inorganic elements, the difficulty would only be removed backward: we should still be the slaves of our elements, and the mystery would lie in them. And analysis, however subtle, must still shrink abashed from the old-world questions—

"Gavest thou the goodly wings unto the peacock? or wings and feathers unto the ostrich?"

"Hast thou given the horse strength? hast thou clothed his neck with thunder?"

"Doth the hawk fly by thy wisdom, and stretch her wings toward the south?"

"Doth the eagle mount up at thy command, and make her nest on high?"

No, brethren; modern analysis, however much it may have widened our vision, has not, cannot bring us one step nearer to the secret of the beginnings of life. For that we must fall back as ever upon the Word, Who has Himself declared to us, "I am the Life;" and if you wonder that He the Life should destroy the swine, and curse the fig-tree, and accomplish His life-giving purpose through the means of a struggle for existence, remember that He clothes the lilies, and watches the falling sparrow, and pities the cattle that are in sinful Nineveh, and be content with His assurance, "It is I; be not afraid."

Once more, as sensibility passes into thought, we rise to the life of man, to which all else was but the prelude.

> "Man, the consummation of this scheme
> Of being, the completion of this sphere
> Of life, whose attributes had here and there
> Been scattered o'er the visible world before,
> Asking to be combined, dim fragments meant

> To be united in some wondrous whole,
> Imperfect qualities throughout creation
> Suggesting some one creature yet to make,
> Some point where all those scattered rays should meet
> Convergent in the faculties of man."

As before, the old lives survive—the lives of force, and growth, and feeling, but elevated, consecrated, crowned by the light of reason, which transfigures force into will, and growth into creativeness, and feeling into love. Man is what he is, willing, creating, loving, by virtue of his reason; and the life of reason is the especial communication of the Word.

"In Him was life, and that life was the light of men;" the light in which we see light; the light of reason "sealed upon us." And all the life of will in the hero, and the statesman, and the conqueror—lifting up the hands which hang down and the feeble knees, undoing the heavy burdens, and letting the oppressed go free, executing judgment and justice in the earth— and all the free creativeness that moulds families, and states, and nations, and laws, and sciences, and literature, and poetry, and art—

and all the life of love in which, by a thousand various channels, the spirit is for ever yearning to return to GOD Who gave it—is possible only through the sustaining omnipresence of the Word. And if you are tempted to see in secular life, or secular study, or civilisation, or in the secular element which is now inwoven with Christianity itself, anything which, evil apart, you think intrinsically common or unclean, recall to mind that all the life of it is due to the inspiration of Him Who, in whatever form appearing, still proclaims across the waters, "It is I; be not afraid." While, on the other hand, where evil is present, whether in the national or individual life, there is the unutterably awful thought, that the powers which He sustains in being are perverted and misused against Him. He is coming to His own, and His own are receiving Him not; and yet He is the Life.

But the process of development does not end with the life of reason. Once more beyond the natural towers the supernatural life, in which again the lower lives of force, of growth, of sense, of reason, are gathered up, transfigured, glorified by personal union with the Word made flesh. "I am the Life," and "Because I live, ye shall live also."

And yet, when we speak of the supernatural life, we are at once confronted by objections. "Hitherto," men say to us, "you have moved in the region of experience and observation; but now you are transcending the limits of evidence and the bounds of common-sense. The very name of the supernatural carries its own condemnation with it; for all that is known or ever can be known by our present faculties is natural. The supernatural is a fiction of the past."

And yet, brethren, if you sweep away these paltry confusions of language you will find there is every whit as much, and as conclusive, evidence for the life of grace as for the life of nature. First, there is the evidence of universal analogy; for every stage in the life of nature is supernatural to that below. Chemistry is supernatural when compared with the life of mechanism; vegetation is supernatural when compared with the life of chemistry; and animal is supernatural to vegetal, and rational to animal life. And if we divided these great classes into their various component portions, we should still find the same order obtaining among their parts. The whole analogy of evolution therefore is in favour of a supernatural life. And, brethren, in saying this I am not playing upon words, or using the word supernatural in two opposite or different senses ; for those who deny the divine presence in the earlier stages of creation, the word " supernatural " is practically equivalent to " contranatural." But the creed of Christendom has never used it in any so irrational a meaning. For the Christian, recognising GOD at the beginning of the series, regards nature and the supernatural as differing (if on such a matter I may use a popular distinction) in degree, but not in kind. I repeat therefore that universal analogy is in favour of a supernatural life.

But we have far stronger evidence than that of mere analogy in the direct testimony of its possessors ; *i.e.* of the only body of men who are qualified by experience to give testimony at all in such a matter. For *experto credite* is a maxim that has no exceptions. You would not ask a mechanician the details of chemistry, nor a chemist those of zoology, nor a zoologist those of policy, any more than an African traveller questions of American geography. Ask the saints, and the virgins, and the martyrs, and the holy and humble men of heart, and the great multitude whom no man can number that have washed their robes and made them white, by what power they wrought righteousness, and quenched the violence of fire, and out of weakness were made strong, and they will tell you, by faith in the power of the supernatural life of grace. And if you still want further evidence, ask your own hearts what is the meaning of their utter inability to find rest, even in the brightest, the most glorious possible phases of the merely natural life; or what is the meaning of the secret misery of unrepented sin, except that it is a poison to the atmosphere which your spirit is gasping to breathe. And so the bitter negative witness of your own hearts and minds and consciences, conspires with the analogies of nature and the testimony of experience, to draw you by a threefold cord of cumulative evidence upward and onward to the supernatural life of grace.

Brethren, of the character and methods of that life it is not my object now to speak to you, but simply of the fact of it, and its harmony with the rest of nature. For before the week is over Lent will be upon us; and Lent, not only from its intrinsic character, but even from the time of its occurrence, is a shock to the natural man. Many of you must have read, in the touching biography of Maurice de Guerin of his going into the fields one Friday in April, and "delighting himself with the shapes of the clouds and the progress of the spring, till he suddenly remembers that it is Good Friday, and exclaims in his diary, 'My GOD, what is my soul about that it can thus go running after such fugitive delights on Good Friday, on this day all filled with Thy death, and our redemption?' And again, 'Of what, my GOD, are we made, that a little verdure and a few trees should be enough to rob us of our tranquillity, and to distract us from Thy love?'"

Such language may be a little foreign, but the experience is universal, either in a finer or a coarser form. There is a strangeness, a collision, a harsh unqualified antagonism between the buoyancy of youth and spring-time, and the thoughts of sin and penitence; growing more and more unbearable as the weeks drag wearily on; the fair earth gathering brightness, and the Lenten shadow deepening, as we draw nearer to the agony in the garden and the voices from the Cross.

We are now in the presence of this conflict, and must all in our measure feel it, whether with the intention of keeping Lent or no. And it is for this reason that I have dwelt to-day upon the deep underlying unity which animates all phases of the development of life. For it is a thought that may, if you will, be a fruitful one for all of you, whatever be your present attitude towards the approach of Lent.

Some of you perhaps have never yet kept, and have no intention of keeping, Lent in any sense or degree whatever. And your reasons may be various; but you will find that they all involve a tacit or a conscious preference of the life of nature to the life of grace. It may be simply the life of sense, in one form or another, the mere animal joy of living, that attracts you; or it may be the life of artistic or literary culture; or it may be the life of human sympathy, the enthusiasm of humanity; or even the more specious pretext of contentment with natural religion. But in whatever shape it is that you prefer the life of nature, remember that you are going backward—you are counterworking your own development—you are perverting, abusing, desecrating the forces of the universe, against the very GOD Who the while sustains them in their being, and is their Life —you are on a course, of which sooner or later the awfully consistent issue will be the calling upon the mountains to fall upon you, and upon the hills to cover you—only to find yourselves flying from the sword and taking refuge in the scabbard, in useless appeal from one power to another of the self-same GOD. Those of you, on the other hand, who, in however small a measure, are still at least desirous of living the supernatural life, remember that there is, there can be, no collision between the GOD of nature and the GOD of grace. And when natural appetites, natural instincts, natural reason, natural affection, are rising in thousand-fold temptation against your higher, truer interests, take comfort from the memory that the same great law of sacrifice is present everywhere throughout the length and breadth of the creation—each being laying down its own as the indispensable condition of receiving a larger life—and be assured that He Who has thus worked hitherto, sustaining, expanding, quickening, developing nature, from strength to strength —is but saying, through the Lenten voices, " Friend, go up higher."

VI.

THE COMMINATION SERVICE.

"My God, my God, look upon me; why hast Thou forsaken me?"—PSALM xxii. 1.

BRETHREN, among the many formulæ which men now claim to have outgrown, the service which we are performing stands prominently forward. Such phrases as "the Primitive Church," "godly discipline," "dangerous days," strike upon the modern ear as little else than curious archaisms, and the thoughts which they embody seem more old-fashioned still. For now-a-days, men say, we do not curse our father or our mother, or remove our neighbour's landmark, or pervert the judgment of the fatherless, or make the blind to go out of his way; and even if our neighbour could commit such antiquarian offences, we should certainly not, on our part, be guilty of the bad taste of cursing him. The service is, in fact, an interesting survival of the Elizabethan age, but does not come quite in contact with the realities of nineteenth century life.

Such criticism is in the air, and you cannot wholly have escaped from it as you listened to the language of the commination service; and with a suspicion of unreality attaching to the great major premiss of Lent, you will not accord much value to its conclusions. I would remind you, therefore, that there are feelings and instincts in human nature, the very antiquity of whose expression is a proof of their universal reality. We translate them from language to language, but they still remain the same,—the touch of nature that makes the whole world kin,—and their meaning is intensified, and their hold upon us strengthened, by the record that other ages felt and thought of them as we think and feel. And foremost among such instincts is the aching sense of severance between man and the Infinite Being outside and above himself. Long before the Hebrew psalmist,

Indians and Egyptians, and savage races beyond the pale of even primitive civilisation, had been, with varying accents, uttering the same lament. And Greek tragedians, and Roman stoics, and mediæval monks and mystics, and all the many voices of modern poets and philosophers, have been echoing incessantly, with however strange a dissonance, the eternal cry of humanity.

"My God, my God, look upon me; why hast Thou forsaken me, and art so far from my health, and from the words of my complaint? Oh, my God! I cry in the daytime, but Thou hearest not; and in the night-season also, I take no rest. And Thou continuest holy, Oh Thou worship of Israel!"

Brethren, it is upon this universal sense of severance, that the spiritual life of Christianity depends, and I am confident that, if you examine yourselves, every one of you will find that, explicitly or implicitly, consciously or instinctively, in one form or another, you feel this severance and want. You may never have dreamed of saying to yourself, "My soul is athirst for God, yea, even for the living God," but you are athirst for finite objects, with a thirst which, upon analysis, will turn out to be infinite, both in quantity and kind, and which, therefore, nothing short of an infinite object can ever satisfy.

Take, for instance, your desire for communion with the natural world. From a child you have desired to acquire more and more of it for your property; to sweep it into the net of your personality; to make the whole of it your own. Social necessity has checked, but never satisfied, this appetite, and you turn unwillingly from the thought of material possession, to content yourself with the spiritual appropriation of the world. But, there too, you are disappointed, for as you gaze upon the woods and mountains, and sea, and sun, and stars, you thirst for a closer communion with them, than sight or thought can give. You wish to be dissolved and lose yourself, and grow incorporate with nature. You desire infinite possession of, and infinite communion with, the grandeur, and the beauty, and the wonder of the world. And failing, you feel bitterly that it is your prison, and not your home.

It is the same with your human relations. You need no authority of Greek philosopher, or Hebrew lawgiver, to assure you that it is not good for man to be alone. For the earliest instinct in your nature tells you so. In childhood and boyhood you are ever seeking for companionship, restless to be reflected in the ways and wills of others; and thus, as you grow older, you thirst for more than mere companionship, and the animal gregariousness of boyhood becomes sympathy, affection, love. And still man will not be satisfied with family, or friendship, or acquaintance. Fresh vistas of humanity are ever opening before him, and each new friend or acquaintance becomes a new point of departure for the extension of his influence to a wider circle still. His motive may be self-sacrifice, or the enthusiasm of humanity, or the selfish love of influence, or the vulgarer forms of ambition. But however the motive may vary, the impulse remains the same; and is simply the instinct to wider, deeper, more intense communion with our fellow-men. And yet, as before, its very unrest is but the measure of its failure. We are cut off by walls and bars from our nearest and our dearest, we can only conjecture their real character, and communicate by signs with them; we cannot be morally, spiritually, physically, one with them, crave it however madly, however sinfully, we will. Much less can we have such absolute intimate communion with the millions upon millions of loving, sorrowing humanity, for which our social instinct in its higher moments yearns. We are more severed from humanity than ever we were from external nature; and if the world is our prison, our fellow-men are our gaolers.

And so in our loneliness we look within, and try to find refuge in an ideal world. But only to find schism and severance in the recesses of our inmost being. Our ideals may be very diverse,—ideals of pleasure, ideals of usefulness, ideals of knowledge, ideals of ambition, ideals of virtue, ideals of love—but all are alike in being above us, and out of our reach. The more we struggle after them, the farther they retreat from us; and when at last, in very weariness, we close our eyes to shut them out, their phantoms are still within us, taunting, mocking, haunting us, with visions of possible pleasure, that only intensify our misery and possible achievement, that only magnify our impotence, and truth, and love, and holiness that only blast by their excess of light. We are farther off from our ideals than even from nature or mankind. They haunt us like an evil conscience, in our imprisoned solitude destroying peace.

Brethren, in moments of reflection you must all have felt already something of this loneliness and isolation from the whole great universe, in one or another of its aspects of appeal to you; and, as life goes on, those moments of reflection will grow more frequent, and their sadness more unbearable, till they end in the moral suicide of cynicism or despair. All this is simply a fact, and a fact as universal as human experience; and Christianity, beyond other creeds, has faced and interpreted the fact.

Some of you may know what it is to meet a friend after long absence, and find your mutual relations changed. You are met at first by a look in the eye, and a tone in the voice, and a touch in the hand, which chill you for a moment with a sense of disappointment. But you hope it is accidental, and will pass away in conversation, only to find in conversation your thoughts, and wills, and plans diverging; till at last you begin to realise that your friend, as a person, has ceased to love you, and that all the other changes were symptoms of a central isolation. It is the same with the Christian account of the human sense of solitude. Nature, and society, and the thoughts of our hearts, were created by a Person, and created for Himself. And the Person who created them, dwells in, and sustains them, and by the fact of His indwelling, makes them the modes of His manifestation; His look, His touch, His voice, the expression of His thought and will. And hence our feelings of separation from the world and its inhabitants, and even from the inner vision of our own ideal self, are but symptoms of alienation from the person in whom they subsist.

"Earth, these solid stars, this weight of body and limb,
Are they not sign and symbol of thy division from Him?
Dark is the world to thee : thyself art the reason why :
For is He not all but thou, that hast power to feel, I am I?
Glory about thee, without thee ; and thou fulfillest thy doom,
Making Him broken gleams, and a stifled splendour and gloom."

Yes, we are persons face to face with an infinite eternal person, and union with Him is the satisfaction to which all our cravings tend. Nor is this a contradiction of the common modern statement that God must be conceived of as "transcending" personality. Of course, the High and Holy One that inhabiteth eternity, whose thoughts are not our thoughts, nor His ways our ways, must transcend all notions that we can form of personality, as the heaven transcends the earth ; but, in transcending, He includes them as vital include chemical functions, or as human includes animal life. We need not, therefore, stop to speculate on what God may be more than personal. It suffices for our present purpose that He is, at least, a person. If He were merely a name for the uniformity of nature, it would be enough that we should live in the fear of, and obedience to, natural law. Or if, again, He were the last resultant of the common or the philosophic consciousness, it would be enough that, to fear and obedience, we should add a moderate philanthropy. Or if, further, He were the aggregate of all possible ideals, it would still be enough that we should celebrate Him in a worship of art and song. But because He is a person, He cannot be contented with the abstracted allegiance of one department of our nature. He claims our being in its wholeness, and says, " Thou shalt love the Lord thy God."

The command, brethren, I admit, is, on the face of it, a paradox, for love is, above all things, essentially and utterly free. But obey, give God your love, and the paradox will pass into a truism, for you will find that you possess Him in whom all things lovely have their being. In union with Him you will no longer feel apart from your ideals, for He is the supreme reality whom all your ideals reflect, and as you go on from strength to strength of power, of usefulness, of influence, of holiness, of purity, of loveliness, of love, the light of your ideal will cease to shine star-like above you, making the darkness visible from its place in the far-off sky; it will pass into your very being, to transfigure and to glorify, till, from shining as light in the world, you are taken to shine as the stars for ever.

Nor will you any longer remain apart from your fellow-men. For, instead of wandering round their prison-house in a vain impotence of longing, straining eyes that cannot see them, and stretching hands that cannot reach them, and calling them with voices which they never understand, you will possess them with a possession unharmed by death or distance through union with Him whose presence is intimate within them, and in whom they live, and move, and die, and have their being.

And, at unity with yourself and in communion with your neighbour, you will no longer feel strange and outcast from the face of the natural world. For in His hand are all the corners of the earth, and the strength of the hills is His also. The sea is His and He made it, and His hands prepared the dry land. If you climb up into heaven, He is there. If you go down to hell, He is there also. If you take the wings of the morning and remain in the uttermost parts of the sea, even there also shall His hand lead you, and His right hand shall hold you.

Such union through God with the universe, and through the universe with God, and therein the sole and perfect satisfaction of your being, is promised you to-day if you will recognise, in your sense of isolation, evidence that you have alienated the love of God by sin.

"Then shalt thou call, and the Lord shall answer; thou shalt cry, and He shall say, Here I am.

"Then shall thy light rise in obscurity, and thy darkness be as the noon-day. And the Lord shall guide thee continually, and satisfy thy soul in drought, and make fat thy bones; and thou shalt be like a watered garden, and like a spring of water, whose waters fail not. . . . For the mouth of the Lord hath spoken it."

Brethren, if internal sophistry, or some eccentric modern theories, or the two in combination, plead that sin is a delusion, remember that sin alone will account for the facts we have been reviewing, and that such has been the verdict of the greatest and wisest of mankind; and, instead of setting our commination service complacently aside, as out of date, hear in it an echo of the ageless, timeless, universal voice of conscience, warning us that, after all, we are no better than our fathers for committing the oldest sins the newest kind of ways, and calling us, as it once called them, to enter His rest who is our peace.

"Our FATHERS hoped in Thee, THEY trusted in Thee, and Thou *didst* deliver THEM.

"THEY called upon Thee, and were holpen; THEY put their trust in Thee and were NOT confounded.

"Be not Thou far from ME, O Lord! Thou art MY succour, haste Thee to help ME."

VII.

PENITENCE.

"Her sins, which are many, are forgiven; for she loved much."
ST. LUKE vii. 47.

FROM the doctrine that God is Personal, and as personal the object of love, flows the unique character of the Christian as against other forms of penitence. For other moral systems tell us that the only true repentance consists simply and entirely in amendment of life for the future, and that all the energy which, instead, is spent in sorrow for the past, is merely a waste of labour that might be otherwise employed. "The only true repentance," says a great philosopher, "is moral amendment." "All sorrow," says another, "is a passage to lesser perfection," and popular opinion has made the same thought familiar in a variety of proverbial forms. But still, the Christian Church, in her age-long ministry to the souls of men, has gained a deeper, truer insight into the springs of human action, than is possible to speculative thinkers or to average men of the world. And as the result of her experience, she proclaims repentance based on sorrow, as not only far truer, but far more fruitful in noble practice, because born of the great desire to atone for wounded love. Analyse your own hearts, my brethren, and ask if there is any motive there so utterly all-powerful as the indignation with yourself, if ever you have wilfully wounded one who loves you, and whom you love; and then look round upon history, and count if you can the deeds of daring, and the willing sacrifices, and the patient sufferings, which, the whole world over, that motive has animated, and inspired, and sustained; and you will no longer think the Christian Church has been unwise in her generation, in calling men to repentance, because they have rejected love.

Sorrow, then, or contrition is the beginning of all true repentance, and the problem of the life of penitence is how contrition may be gained. God, men say, though we believe in Him, seems very far away from us, and the sufferings of the cross are past and over long ago. There is no present object to help me realise that I have wounded the love of God.

My brethren, go back to the history recorded in my text, and see what kind of love it was which there merited forgiveness. That poor woman in her misery did not know that she was worshipping the everlasting Son of the Father, very God of very God. Only, she had watched the prophet of Nazareth in Galilee, as He went about doing good in the streets and lanes of her sinful city. She had caught somewhat of the far-off meaning of the deep sorrow in His eyes, as He looked round upon men, and was grieved at the hardness of their hearts. She had listened to His stern rebuke of the complacent hypocrites in their high places—to His invitation of the heavy-laden, and His blessing on the pure in heart. And she felt as she looked and listened, that there was a presence in humanity, on which her life of sin had been an outrage and a shame; and in the rock-like shelter of that presence, overshadowing the weary world, the faded instincts of her true womanhood revived and blossomed into action —and her sins, which were many, were forgiven her; for she loved much.

Brethren, we are not bold enough in realising how true it is that the knowledge of God must be learned inductively from His presence among men. Even when another church, or an alien system of philosophy, brings this truth before us with more than usual emphasis, we view it with suspicion, as being a questionable novelty, forgetting that all the while it has stared us in the face, in the plain unmistakable language of the disciple whom Jesus loved. "Thou shalt love the Lord thy God with all thy heart, and with all thy mind, and with all thy soul, and with all thy strength," and "Thou shalt love thy neighbour as thyself," are not two independent and separate commandments; they are involved, and contained in, and presuppose each other— and to St. John's mind they were one.

"Every one that loveth is born of God, and

knoweth God;" "No man hath seen God at any time. If we love one another, God dwelleth in us, and His love is perfected in us." "He that loveth not his brother, whom he hath seen, how CAN he love God, whom he hath not seen?" "And this commandment have we from Him, That he who loveth God, love his brother also."

All this is only saying that the spiritual region is subject, like all others, to the universal law of knowledge, which tells us that we must begin with the observation of what lies round about us, and pass, step by step, from the facts of experience to the great principles on which they rest. And if you would only bear this in mind in its application to the spiritual life, you would soon find that your contrition became real.

Begin by thinking of your friends, and you will find that each of them, with all his faults, still has the advantage of you in some quality of virtue. One is more truthful, another more self-sacrificing, another more conscientious, another more industrious, another kinder, another humbler, another purer than yourself.

Each has made some effort or use of opportunities, and therefore become in some faint measure a channel of grace to the souls of others, while you have remained fruitless, cumbering the ground. And in proportion as it is so you must feel unworthy of their love.

Then go on to think of all the unknown human beings who have toiled, and are toiling, with head, and heart, and hand, to furnish you with your material, moral, intellectual endowments—the noble souls that have contended for the law and liberty which you enjoy; and the martyrs, and the missionaries, and the long line of saints and heroes, who have laboured to hand on to you the faith which now you hold so cheap, while you have been seeking your own pleasure, day by day, and year by year, without a thought of the uncounted sorrows which have gone to make that pleasure possible,—setting an example which, however negative, must go out beyond yourself and seduce others into habits, at least of indolence and carelessness, if not of the more actively antisocial kinds of sin, and so by your own life and that of those whom you have influenced, bequeathing to after ages an accumulated legacy of ill. For when you see a strong man struggling helpless against unfair odds, and dying prematurely, outworn in the cause of good, and unsuccessful, remember it is not the men of his own generation who have killed him, but the stubborn, dull resistance of sloth, and apathy, and selfishness, which the sins of successive ages have gone on building, inch by inch, into the forms of our society and the very fabric of the world. And such is the fate which your sins are entailing on generations yet unborn.

With these thoughts in your minds, brethren, look back to the cross of Calvary, and you will, I think, no longer see there the empty symbol of a suffering now long past and over, in the grave, where all things are forgotten, but the inner meaning and reality of the age - long passion of humanity, in the crucifixion of Him who all along has been an hungred, and you gave Him no meat ; thirsty, and you gave Him no drink; a stranger, and you took Him not in ; naked, and you clothed Him not ; sick and in prison, and you visited Him not; and who still pleads, from our streets, and hospitals, and prisons, and haunts of sinful misery, and from all the coasts of heathendom perishing in darkness: "Is it nothing to you, all ye that pass by? Behold, and see if there be any sorrow like unto my sorrow." And, gradually, as you behold Him your contrition will become more real.

And though contrition is only, as I have said, the first part of penitence, it is one of those halves that contains, in itself, the whole. For real contrition must express itself, first in word and then in deed; and so it leads us onward to confession and satisfaction. It must do so if it is real, for all real thought or feeling burns impatiently within us till it has clothed itself in language. Thought and feeling, which has not yet come forth into contact with the outer world, is still, in a measure, abstract, indefinite, unreal; and therefore, the contrition which comes of knowing that we have wounded love, must, in proportion to its intensity, thirst for utterance in words—out of the fulness of the heart the mouth speaking. And yet, it has been said with terrible truth, in a popular attack upon modern Christianity, that the language of our public confessions is rather rhetorical than real,—a tale of little meaning though the words be strong. When you say—or kneel quiescent, and allow others to say for you—that you have erred and strayed like lost sheep, that you have followed too much the devices and desires of your own hearts, that you have offended against God's holy laws, that you have left undone those things which you ought to have done, and have done those things which you ought not to have done, and the remembrance of all this is grievous unto you, and the burden of it intolerable, and that there is no health in you,—do you use these awful words with their full weight of meaning in them, or have they dwindled into formulæ which you do not even construe into thought? If the latter, make an effort to view confession as gathering up and investing your contrition with the reality of the spoken word, remembering, when you make it publicly, that you are members one of another, and have sinned against your brethren, and through and in the persons of your brethren, against the Son of man, who is the Son of God, and against your Father which is in heaven; and realising, if you make it privately, that the root and essence of all your sin is alienation from the divine love, and therefore from the human.

"Against THEE only have I sinned, and done this evil in THY sight."

"My lovers and friends hast THOU put away from me, and hid mine acquaintance out of my sight."

But Mary was not contented with contrition and confession. She brake the box of ointment, and poured it on His feet. Words are more real than thoughts, and therefore confession than contrition; but deeds are more real than words, and we have sinned in the region of action, and therefore our repentance must go one step farther and become fact. And so important is this third element in the life of penitence, that, as we saw at starting, there have been thinkers who mistook it for the whole. Satisfaction is not the whole, but it is the crown and goal of penitence, whether it comes in the form of action, or of suffering, or of both. And to make your satisfaction real, think again of the great human brotherhood, and in the points in which you have wronged it resolve to make your amends,

Take the time which is still before you, whether it be short or long, and think how others, though in the flesh unknown to you, still of like passions with yourselves,—with the same sense of incapacity, the same hunger for enjoyment, the same temptation to fold the hands in apathetic indolence,—have arisen and denied themselves, and shaken off their sloth, and set their faces sternly to work and to labour till their evening, that you, in the distant future, might enter into the fruit of their labours, and resolve to atone, in the days to come, for the time you have squandered in the past.

Then take your capacities, whether of body or of mind, and think how many of your fellows, with the same flood of impetuous passion surging in their veins, and the same importunate temptation to dissipate life in sensuality, and drown its bitter after-thoughts in the wine-cup and the opiate, have disciplined and husbanded their health, and strength, and energy, to leave you the gathered fruits of it, and all its memory of great example; and think how others at this moment, without possibility of choice, are wearing out health and life in the pleasureless mines, and towns, and factories, to provide you with the necessities, the comforts, the luxuries of life; and as you think of all these, and their doings, and their sufferings for you, and the small good and the much evil which you, in your turn, have done to others, determine to preserve your strength and energy by temperance, and soberness, and chastity, and to dedicate your future to the service of mankind.

Then recall the intellectual servants of your race,—the poets, who have felt, and suffered, and "learned in sorrow what they taught in song;" the philosophers, who have wrestled painfully with the great problems of existence to make the life of others seem a little less forlorn; the men of science who have laboured on, with untiring industry and life-long patience, to enrich mankind with some small fragment of the knowledge which is power; and the moralists, and prophets, and teachers, who, themselves weary and outworn, have still cheered, and sustained, and comforted their travel-worn companions with hopes of the promised land, and the day when the wilderness should blossom as the rose. Think, as you remember these, of all the powers and opportunities which you have wasted, and are wasting here, in the central home of thought, and resolve to bear your share also in the thorn-crowned work of intellect.

And then think of the long catalogue we so often recite in Oxford, of the founders and the benefactors who have served us with their wealth, endowing universities, colleges, churches, museums, galleries, libraries, hospitals, alms-giving societies, for the blessing of generations which they themselves had never seen. We pass over their names lightly when praising famous men; but be sure that in their day they were among those who loved much, and think how you too, in your measure, may, by imitating, repay their love: it may be by using their endowment fruitfully, it may be by providing for the poor and needy, it may be by the offering of costly ointment, but it must be by remembering that your wealth, whencesoever derived, is not yours to do what you like with, but to be given to the angel money-changers, that the Son of man may receive His own with usury.

If these, and such as these, brethren, are the motives to your "satisfaction," you will not need to add to them other modes of penitential pain, for you will come to know, increasingly, how "doing" and "suffering" are one, and that your every action for humanity is a part of its great passion, and that whenever the few years of your activity are over, and the night of your pain and sorrow drawing on, your suffering is only a still higher form of action, helping others by its merits, its patience, its example; and so, in a faint and far-off measure, atoning for the love that you have wronged. For, when the

Son of man shall come in His glory, he shall say unto you, "Inasmuch as ye have done it unto the least of these My brethren, ye have done it unto Me."

VIII.

KNOWLEDGE.

"If any man will do His will, he shall know of the doctrine."
ST. JOHN vii. 17.

THERE is a tendency in every age to make the most of its own sum of evil, and one of the evils which now-a-days we often hear exaggerated is the alienation of our intellect from our faith. But there have lived brave men before and after Agamemnon; and no race or generation can claim a monopoly of disbelief, scepticism, materialism, pantheism, each of them in turn professed to be the last word of Greek and Roman civilisation. And when ancient society gave way before the Christian spirit and the northern blood, the world exchanged the cynicism of decadence for the heresies of youth; and gained "for a life of doubt diversified by faith, a life of faith diversified by doubt." The creeds and canons of the early Church were distilled from the waters of bitter controversy, and throughout the centuries which some men are fond of calling the dark ages, and others the ages of faith ; the masses, as we gather, lived on in a superstition of which only the name was changed—while higher in society there were sceptical opinions, and courtiers made infidel epigrams, and men of science were atheistic, and the cloister gave asylum for nonconformity of religious thought. The Renaissance only published what for ages the world had been thinking, and the last three centuries have only developed what was contained in the Renaissance.

"Say not thou," therefore, "what is the cause that the former days were better than these?" Of course the ages fluctuate in their vices as well as in their virtues, but through all the fluctuations there is a sense in which history repeats itself, and it is of real use that from time to time we should be reminded, for our consolation, that in our collective as truly as in our individual life, there hath no temptation taken us but such as is common to man. And the reason for all this is that so-called intellectual error springs, as a rule, from other than purely intellectual sources. It is part and parcel of the perversion of our whole personality, and to think otherwise is to be the victim of our language, and to imagine that because, for convenience in speaking, we divide human nature into so many senses, and emotions, and an intellect, and a will, it is not all the while one simple, entire, undecomposable whole. Precisely as you cannot separate your emotions from your reason, and feel a single appetite, which is not more than merely animal, so neither can you separate your reason from your emotions, and prevent your wish, however obscurely, from being father to your thought. Aristotle and Bacon, and the late J. Stuart Mill, are the last thinkers who could ever be accused of obscurantism. Yet they are all equally emphatic in asserting that the causes of fallacy are partly moral. Analyse your personality, and you will feel that it must be so; be honest with your conscience, and you will feel that it is so. Take, for example, sloth, and omitting the more obvious impediments which it casts in the way of your intellectual attainment, such as oversleep, idleness, disproportionate amusement; think in how many subtler forms it enters into and dulls the use of the intellectual faculties. There is the sloth which refuses to grapple and wrestle with the truth, and which leads those who are by nature more intellectual than conscientious, to be satisfied with skimming curiously through a number of books; and these who, on the other hand, are more conscientious than intellectual, to be content with unintelligent plodding through a stated number of hours,—in either case degrading thought, and the truth with which thought deals, into a beggarly thing of quantity, that can be measured by the yard. And then there is the cowardly form of sloth, that shrinks from consequences. You have heard of the value of some religious ordinance, and you decline to think out the question, lest it should prove inconveniently personal. Or you are on the brink of some line of thought which, followed on, may perhaps estrange you from friends, or qualify your allegiance to your party, or your own favourite convictions, or the plan and purpose of your life. And you shrink from such an effort, not from high motives but from sloth. And so, by small degrees, your intellectual insight becomes dimmer, till, with Pilate, you ask, What is truth? and do not wait for an answer. Or again, pride may be your enemy, the pride which, from the vantage-ground of physical strength or beauty, or the circumstances of your social position, or hereditary creed, looks down upon the world of thought as a pale, ghost-like unreality; or the pride which does not despise knowledge, but thinks itself possessed of it, convinced that its own theory, or the theory of its own party, in church or state, or art or literature, is, if not quite exclusively, at least predominantly true. And pride, too, has its fear of consequences. You cannot take rank among kings of thought, and you will not expose yourself to failure;

preferring to reign in a hell of imbecility rather than serve in an intellectual heaven. Or else you cannot bear the supercilious pity of your fellows, when they find you are more dogmatic, or more comprehensive, or more critical, or more conscientious, or more moderate, or more extreme, than their own would-be infallibility; and so you are false to the vision of truth till the vision is taken from you.

Such are some of the ways in which pride and sloth obscure the reason, and you will find upon examination that it is the same with all other sins. Gluttony, drunkenness, impurity, anger, jealousy, sins of the tongue, each in proportion as it becomes habitual, jars all the delicate mechanism of your personality; and puts your understanding out of focus, till you can no longer see the truth.

And remember that here also, as well as in the moral region, your sins go out beyond you, and cause your brother to offend. You may see everywhere around you, great, patient, energetic thinkers, who all their life have " scorned delight, and lived laborious days," and yet remain in alienation from the Christian faith and the Christian hope; and think it uncharitable to attribute their intellectual error to moral causes. You forget the awful fact that moral causes act vicariously, and that it is the sloth, and pride, and bigotry, and unreality of Christians, which causes men to question the divinity of Christ. It is so in the great outer world, and it is so in the circles of college life; and be sure, that if it continue so, in the great day of disillusionment, the men of science and the atheists shall rise in judgment upon our generation, and shall condemn it. For they will have been true to the light they knew of, and you will have been false to a clearer light.

But there is another reason for the union of moral with intellectual truth, over and above there being two aspects of the same human personality. They are aspects of the same divine Personality of God; and to be severed from Him in one, is in a measure to be severed from Him in all His aspects. It is only he that willeth to do who can possibly know of the doctrine, just as we can only understand a friend because we love him, or a science when we pursue it *con amore*. Only " He that loveth is born of God, and knoweth God."

Take a few of those departments of knowledge with which you here are more immediately concerned, and see whether you are using them as instrumental to the knowledge of God. Half the time of all of you is occupied with language. And what is language? It is not summed up and done with, when you have said that words are wise men's counters, but the money of fools. For language is very much more than that. It floats like a great atmosphere, mediating between two worlds, and partaking of either nature, half material, and half spiritual. Flame-like to kindle, and water-like to quench; it is the great beneficent power that links man to man, and age to age, and makes common thought and feeling, and corporate action possible. But it is also a great divider, that separates nation from nation, by barriers which a lifelong labour cannot wholly overpass. And then it invests our thoughts, whether for weal or for woe, with something of its own everlasting terrible reality; carrying our good intentions out, far and wide beyond us, and keeping them alive and powerful, when we ourselves are gone; and wresting our thoughts of evil in a moment from our own keeping, to enter them against us in its register of sin. It is the living book of judgment which, from the dawn of human history, has been silently recording the good and evil done upon earth; that in the day when the books are opened, and the judgment-seat is set, by our words we may be justified, and by our words we may be condemned. And in all this, it is a reflection of the nature and character of Him, who was in the beginning with God, and was God; and yet who was made flesh, and dwelt among us, binding together all kindreds and peoples of the earth into one; but smiting the rebellious nations with the sharp sword that goeth out of his mouth, and choosing among His titles as pre-eminent, the Word. It is the same with history; for history, after all, is more than the catalogue of crimes which it seems to the eye of the cynical historian. History is the great "Theodicy," the record of the way which the Lord our God hath led us, concealing Himself in a cloud of mercy in the day of our prosperity; revealing Himself in a fire of judgment in the night of our desolation; guiding, guarding, inspiring, raising up and casting down, saving, rebuking, punishing, leaving Himself not without witness; making evermore for righteousness. While a man is young he may look back on his life and not see its special providence; but none can read history, in any true sense of the word, without acknowledging, "Verily, there is a reward for the righteous; doubtless there is a God that judgeth the earth." And as of history, so of law; law — which has sunk in these degenerate days into a pretext for illegality, and a synonym for frivolous procrastination. It was otherwise with that law which was given among lightnings upon Sinai, with that "disembodied wisdom," which Greek poets and philosophers invoked, as co-eternal and co-equal with God Himself; that law which invested even the infamy of the Roman decadence with majesty; that law of which "there can be no less acknowledged, than that her throne is the bosom of God and her operation the harmony of the universe." "Lord, what love have I unto Thy law; all the day long is my study in it." "Great is the peace that they have who love Thy law; and they are not offended at it."

It is the same with science, throwing new, and ever newer, light on those ways that are not our ways, and thoughts that are not as our thoughts; with art; with the mysterious mathematical relationships; and above and beyond all with "divine philosophy." Every branch of human knowledge is a channel of communication between the personality of God and the personality of man, and therefore of necessity qualified and altered by the relations of those personalities one to the other. As long as we are alienated from the life of God that is in us, our knowledge may indeed be intellectually accurate, and even fruitful in blessing for others, but it will fall short of its true destiny, which is to point us on to the Beatific vision, to the day when we shall know even as also we are known, and in that knowledge find our peace.

IX.

FAITH.

"Now faith is the substance of things hoped for, the evidence of things not seen."—HEBREWS xi. 1.

AGES, like individuals, have their besetting sins, and prominent among those of the present day is faithlessness. We have many excellent characteristics, without doubt; we should be inhuman if it were not so. We are earnest, after our fashion, enterprising, intellectually veracious, humane, liberal, tolerant; but, underneath, and behind all this, we are emphatically a faithless generation. The one thing conspicuous by its absence from our social and political dealings, from our literature, from our art, from our thought, from the conduct of our lives, is faith; and yet, "whatsoever is not of faith is sin," and "without faith it is impossible to please God."

Brethren, such a statement would need apology, if it were other than a truism, and therefore, if any of you doubt that it is a truism I will ask you to consider for a moment what faith is. We too often think and speak of it as a speculative faculty, co-ordinate with reason, and differing from reason only in being concerned with a different subject-matter; as if, while reason assures us that honesty is the best policy, or that probability is the guide of life, or that the laws of nature are uniform, faith supplies us with similar judgments about God, and spirit, and immortality ;. judgments, *i.e.*, which may or may not have an important bearing upon our lives, but which are exhausted, as far as faith is concerned, by the intelligent recital of the orthodox creed. And in the false security of this convenient error, we see the majority of professing Christians live and listen to the language of Scripture with increased complacency as years go on, thinking the while that however many their other negligences and ignorances, they are at least safe as regards their faith.

But this is not S. Paul's view when he says, "We walk by faith and not by sight," and "Faith is the substance of things hoped for, the evidence of things not seen." Sight, intuition, vision, by whatever name you call it, is a higher thing than reason, for it is that in which reason ends; and faith is higher than even sight, for it is sight become creative. Human sight, like human reason, feeds upon experience, must have an object set before it, cannot work without materials. But faith is independent of experience, and in a way creates its object. It sees in darkness, believes without evidence, is certain of impossibilities, grapples with and forces the blank, dark, empty nothingness, into substance, and consistency, and reality, and life; it is the reflection, almost too bright for frail human nature, of the divine power that can create *ex nihilo*.

Brethren, I will ask you to bear in mind this creative character of faith, and then to look about you and see where it exists.

First, there is the natural world around you, with its beauty, its variety, its harmony, its order, its simplicity of operation, its complexity of result, its myriad contributions to life and health and cheerfulness, its awful, dark, relentless ministries of death. Never before, whether by art or science, were the aspects and the processes of this natural world so curiously, sensitively, lovingly watched as now. And yet the issue of it all is *not* that "the invisible things of God from the creation of the world are clearly seen, being understood by the things that are made, even His eternal power and Godhead." Rather we "have swept the heavens with our telescope and found no God." And the blame of this lies not with our science, but with ourselves. Science, by the necessity of its nature, deals, and ought to deal, only with what is matter of observation—with the things that are seen; and the tendency of a scientific age therefore must inevitably be to overstimulate the sensual and weaken the spiritual imagination. It is we who should be on our guard against this tendency, and indolently are not. We allow its results to pass into our literature and language, till at last they become too strong for us, like the stereotyped phrases of old age. We accustom ourselves to separate the realms of faith and nature; to set primary far apart from secondary causes; to think the physical more uniform than the moral and spiritual order; and gradually, by admitting that there may be reality apart from spirit, to supply premisses for the demonstration that spirit is unreal: while the same process of degradation is meanwhile paralysing our practice, and from the concession that some departments of life may be lived without need of faith, we are led on by an inexorable logic to think faith itself a superfluity. For men, as a rule, are more consistent than they are willing to admit; and the consequence of moral upon intellectual error, which S. Paul has so explicitly and terribly declared, is a necessity, and must appear either in the individual or the race: as many know, who have never dreamed of being troubled by a theory, but in their agony have lent an ear, when some impetuous temptation was upon them, to the whispered suggestion, "After all, may not the philosophers be right when they assure me that I have neither the freedom nor the power for resistance?" Penitence may bring back insight, when the sin is past and over; but, in the interval, intellectual materialism has done its work. The fathers have eaten sour grapes, and the children's teeth are set on edge.

Brethren, the sole remedy for all this is to remember that matter and spirit, as we call them, are but aspects of each other, the reverse and obverse of the same coin, the concavity and convexity of the same circle, the bright and the dark surface of the same God-concealing cloud. And to hold fast this faith in all its applications —to recognise divine attributes in every phase of nature—to trace a network of peculiar providence in the blind evolution of forces—to realise that your bodies are the temples of the Holy Ghost—all this requires an effort which, in the face of modern influences, can be called little less than creative.

And then there are our social surroundings, and they too demand faith, and a faith which as we grow older is less easy to retain—*i.e.* faith in our fellow-men. There is so much that is un-

lovely and repulsive on the surface of society—
so much selfishness, deceit, ingratitude, ignorance,
prejudice, frivolity—and then below the surface
so much evil where we hoped for good, and the
evil seems so persistent, and the good so soon
wears out, that men tend to think less and less
of each other as the years of life go on, and to
speak of each other, and act toward each other,
as little more than " men machines ;" good perhaps, as the world goes, or useful, or agreeable,
but very unfitting objects for enthusiasm, or
reverence, or love. It is a dreary picture, this ;
but your own experience must assure you that
it is a true one, of societies from which youth
and its generosity have passed away. Set aside
your own friends, and those whose friendship
you still wish for : and what then are other men
to you (even in the walls of the same college) ?
Are they not already objects of slightly con-
temptuous indifference, if not actually of open
contempt ? Brethren, what they are now the
rest of your world will in time become to you.
Friendship will pale into acquaintance ; and
acquaintance into estrangement ; bonds of

feeling into bonds of utility; persons into things.

And yet, the while, each human soul of them has been chosen of God in the far eternity, and loved by Him with a peculiar love, and endowed by Him with special graces, and sent earthward with capacities and a destiny all its own; and throughout its days of pilgrimage is being waited on by angels, longing to bid it welcome, at the last,to its eternal home. Realise this by faith, and it will regenerate the world for you. You will cease to judge by the surface, and to impute motives, and to give party-names. You will distinguish the divine essence from the human accretions on a character. Service will win affection from you; acquaintance become friendship; friendship, instead of fading, will gather intensity with time; the vague enthusiasm of humanity that comes and goes in youth capriciously, will strengthen, ripen, fructify, into an abiding love for souls; and as you live and move amid spiritual presences, in worlds not realised before, you will know the blessedness of walking by faith and not by sight. It is an effort—a creative effort, but an effort worth the making.

But if you are to look in this way upon society, you must go further, and carry faith into your view of political life. For political questions have so prominent a place in our ordinary modern life — they form so large a part of our ephemeral reading, and of our superficial culture—and of our conversational stock-in-trade, that we cannot prevent our views of society being leavened by political modes of thought. And this is a fresh danger to our faith. For policy deals with men in masses, and is accustomed, like physical science, to ignore, for its own purposes, the spiritual side of life. At intervals, when some great wave of spiritual emotion sweeps across the current of our international diplomacy, we are awakened to the incongruity between our public practice and our private theory. But, for the most part, out of sight is out of mind. Yet the duties which men have as individuals, they cannot lay aside as nations. Nations have responsibilities, and a conscience, and a destiny, and a time of their visitation, and a judgment to come. We smile at Herodotus for writing history on such a principle; and yet we have the assurance of less fallible historians that national sins, and not commercial or military accidents, were the ruin of Egypt, and Syria, and Tyre, and Persia, and Babylon, and Greece. It was as a nation that the Israelites were chosen, guided, guarded, wept over for not knowing the things which belonged unto their peace. And the nations of Christian Europe, to the Scriptural philosopher of history, have risen, and declined, and fallen, according to their spiritual state. And yet, in our thoughts upon contemporary politics, we seem utterly unconscious of all this. We do not deny it; we simply forget it; and, as the consequence of our forgetfulness, we lapse, little by little, into a low view of collective humanity; which, in its turn, insensibly degrades our habitual estimate of our fellowmen; and then of the world we live in; and then of our very selves. For intellectual materialism, social materialism, political materialism, cannot act, and interact, and react upon each other all around you and leave the personal life unharmed. For the personal life, we are told, consists in a correspondence with its environment, and is the creature of the atmosphere it breathes. You cannot be one person abroad, and another person at home, and separate your religion from the other spheres of your activity, any more than you can serve two masters. The attempt to do so means that you are not yet fully conscious of the claims of either. But, be sure that sooner or later that consciousness *will* come; and then it will be well for you if the faith which guides your inner life should begin slowly and laboriously to reconquer your outer world,—but it is far more probable that the faithlessness which, in your external relations, has been allowed to increase and multiply till it has become almost a form of thought, will then extend its benumbing influence to the last relics of your faith. Such is the too-common history of spiritual as of military defeat. The flank is turned upon a quarter where attack was least expected, and the central defences fall without a blow.

Turn, therefore, lastly, to your personal lives, and see how faith is faring there. Why, when your health, and wealth, and time, and opportunities are not actively misused for evil, are they so often frittered away? Simply for want of faith. You start in life with high ideals, and an exuberance of energy—but you have not courage to bring the two into relation; *i.e.* you have not faith. Your ideals are like the visions that float before the artist; they are unreal to begin with; but you are endowed with a creative faculty, and can call them into existence by the bare fiat of your faith. You can *make* them what they are not—as the heroes and saints have done before you; but you *will* not, and so you allow the God-sent vision of your destiny to fade away unfulfilled, till in the end it will be nothing more to you than the melancholy memory of some sunrise long ago.

It is the same with life's other aspect; its sickness, and pain, and sorrow. It comes to you with a message full of spiritual meaning, but you are not on the look-out for spiritual meaning at the time; even if you are in the habit of looking for it elsewhere, as in the course of human history, or the aspect of the natural world, you suffer the sudden transition to put the eye of your faith out of focus, and fail to recognise spirit when it appears in this new disguise. You busy your thoughts at once with a host of secondary causes; the habit, or place, or indiscretion, which may have brought your illness on you—or the medicine, or diet, or change of air which you hope will soon take it away. You have not the faith to discard all these, and confront the reality which they conceal. You are like Asa, who, "in his disease, sought not to the Lord, but to the physicians." And so the angel that was sent to give you patience, or insight, or recollection, or the one especial grace which was your need, passes away with the heavenly message which he brought you undelivered, and only leaves you one step nearer, but less ready, for your grave. And yet, if you had only known it, "this sickness was not unto death, but for the glory of God, that the Son of God might be glorified thereby."

Such, brethren, in all the relations of their lives, was the character of the faith of that long catalogue of heroes who, "having obtained a good report," "received not the promise,"—and such, brethren, at least must be ours, if they without us are not to be made perfect.

X.

LOVE.

"God is love."—1 St. John iv. 8.

THERE was a controversy in Oxford, not many years ago, as to whether words could be applied in the same sense to things human and divine— whether justice, and love, and jealousy, in God, had the same meaning as among men; and, despite of all intellectual arguments to the contrary — the religious consciousness of all healthy minds instinctively felt that, if religion was to exist at all, words must preserve their identity of meaning to whomsoever they applied; and that to say, for example, that justice meant one thing in man, and another thing in God, was only a cumbrous way of saying that God was, and must remain, unknowable. But though our theory upon the subject may be ever so correct, we tend instinctively, in the practice of life, to shrink from its application, and to empty our language of all human meaning before using it of heavenly things. And in no case is this more striking than when we speak of the "love" of God; and convert a word that, in our earthly intercourse, is full of life, and heart, and fire, into a pale, far-off, indefinite abstraction. I will ask you therefore to analyse what it is that we call "love," with a view to see the meaning of the term when applied to God.

In perfect love there are three elements, which may best be seen by examining the three states of life in which they are respectively most prominent—the filial, the fraternal, the parental.

The first form of love, in the history of each of us, is that of a child to his parent; and, as a rule, it is the weakest form, but it contains and exhibits in an exceptional degree the first and essential element in all true love—reverential trustfulness. There is none of the passion or the sacrifice in a child's feeling for his parents, that will come with after days—but there is a quiet sense of being at home with them, and at peace under their protection,—a vague alarm when we are away from them; and a security when they are present, as of one slumbering in the sunshine. They are *ends* to us, absolute boundaries, beyond which we need not look into the cold outer world; and we possess in our parents, during the few short years of childhood, the spiritual rest which we have seen men afterwards try to create for themselves in vain, in the thought of an infallible Church. This, then, is the first characteristic of love—reverential trustfulness, rest in an end. But with the passing away of childhood a new need dawns upon the spirit of man—the need to be an end, in whom others can rest, as he finds rest in them; the need for reciprocity of affection, such as is found in a brother, a friend, a wife. It is this reciprocity that is, in the common opinion, the chief characteristic of love, and as in all natural reciprocity, so too here, the more distinct are the elements the closer is their union; and in ordinary cases, and for ordinary men, therefore, the love of friend is closer than the love of brother, and the love of woman than the love of friend.

And yet there is a height above the reciprocity of wedded love. Greater love hath no man than this, that a man lay down his life for his friends—the pure self-sacrifice of disinterested love—which I have called parental love, or the parental element in love; because, again speaking of the average of cases and the average of men, it is in parents that such love is oftenest and earliest seen. A mother does not expect, and cannot expect, any adequate return for the time, and care, and thought, bestowed through life upon her children. She reverences them as new lives, new modes of being in the universe, to whom mysteriously she has given birth—she loves them from their hour of weakness to the hour of their strength, and desires that, as far as may be, her love may be reciprocated, but she feels, with every advancing year, that it never may be, it never can be so—that it is their destiny to increase, hers to decrease; and that a man shall leave his father and his mother, not only in his life but also in his love. To feel this, and to accept it, is the perfect sacrifice of maternal love.

Such, then, are the three elements which go to make up love,—reverence, desire, sacrifice—inextricably intertwined into a new something, which is none of them, and yet all of them together—the whiteness of the prism, the trinity in unity of love.

Consequently, if God be Love, that love must exist and be exhibited as possessing in their fulness this trinity of elements; and if to dwell in love be to dwell in God, that love in which we dwell must have its full development, and we must pass, in our spiritual history, from trust through desire to sacrifice, just as in our natural history we pass from filial through wedded to parental love.

"Let no man think that sudden, in a minute,
All is accomplished, and the work is done.
Though with thine earliest dawn thou shouldst begin it,
Scarce were it ended in thy setting sun."

The failure to recognise the life of love as one of thus gradual development has been the great cause of erroneous teaching and erroneous living in the world, by leading teachers to look impatiently for disinterested love,—the love of sacrifice, where God only intended its earlier stages to exist—and their hearers to conclude, by an inevitable logic, that if the God of the theologians had placed them in a world of loveliness simply and solely that they might not love it, theologians must be using words in their non-natural senses, and God is love must mean God is hate. And yet, from the very beginning of all Christian theology two sentences had plainly stared men in the face. Plato had said, " The true order of approaching to the things of love is to use the beauties of earth as steps along which to mount upward to that other beauty, rising from the love of one to the love of two, and from the love of two to the love of all fair forms, and from fair forms to fair deeds, and from fair deeds to fair thoughts, till from fair thoughts he reaches on to the thought of the Uncreated loveliness, and at last knows what true beauty is." And St. John had said : " If a man love not his brother, whom he hath seen, how *can* he love God, whom he hath not seen ?"

The beginning of the dwelling in love, therefore, is to love the things that we have seen—earth, and the sea, and the stars, and forms of flowers, and twilight on the hills, and the song of birds and the quick glancing life of the animals, and the strength and the passion and the beauty of woman and of man; and then the great world of art, in which man has caught, and focused, and reflected back on earth, the light of her own loveliness intensified a thousand-fold; the sculpture of Athens, and Italian painting, and the music of our modern world; and then, lastly, the fair thoughts with which science has enriched us, of the history and destiny of our world and our race. It is in the loving of all such things that we learn what it is to love. Our folly and sin is to darken our eyes to them and deny that they are lovely. And if in your hatred of this sinfulness you have fallen into its opposite, and too long loved earth only for its earthly sake, remember that with the capacity for the false love goes the capacity for the true, and think of her who, after all her sinfulness, was preferred to a Pharisaic priesthood and a Sadducean society "because she loved much." The sin is in mistaking a part for the whole, and stopping short in our career of progress. For all these finite things of beauty are still but the steps that Plato speaks of, and cannot for ever satisfy the heart of man with all its infinite capacities. But this, the one fact which preachers so much insist upon, is surely the very fact that least needs such insistance. For it is a matter of only too frequent and everyday experience. Weakness comes, and with it weariness, and the glory passes from the earth; and death isolates us, and friends are faithless, and art and science lose their magic to charm the desolated heart; till most men are ready at last to echo as their own the words of Job:

"The mountain falling cometh to nought, and the rock is removed out of his place, the waters wear the stones, thou washest away the things which grow of the dust of the earth, and thou destroyest the hope of man."

But this is only the beginning of the second stage of love, for out of the very fact of this hope destroyed it is that there springs the passionate cry, "Whom have I in heaven but thee? and there is none upon earth that I desire in comparison of thee." Man tires of his toys; he cannot be for ever gazing on the face of a nature from which comes no response; the forms of art are soon exhausted, and science is too slow for the impatience of his questioning; and the more passionately he loves his fellows the more he feels that none nor all of them are adequate to satisfy his capacities for love. He feels that there is room in his heart for the love of the infinite universe, and cannot rest till the great Infinite reciprocates his love.

But it is only through having known the earthly love in its intensity that such a man has come to learn the greatness of his own capacities, by having gone through it all, and found that there were abysses still beyond it— by having gathered it all in and garnered it, and found that there was still room for more.

"Nor man nor nature satisfies whom God alone created."

It is no longer but the peace of the child in

the presence of its father. It is the passion for the bridegroom of the bride.

"Like as the hart desireth the water brooks, so longeth my soul after Thee, O God."

Then, but not till then, will love enter upon its highest stage and put on the crown of sacrifice, for sacrifice is the language of love, its only adequate expression, its last effort of the spirit, whom no union with the object of its love can satisfy short of the self-annihilation that shall make that object all in all.

This is a goal very far from us—the love of saints—the love of the men whom God in His turn *reverences*—but it has been realised, by one and another lonely soul, along the ages— living afar, upon the mountains, in the air we cannot breathe, to remind us that, after all, sacrifice is an element in love—and an element that will be present in proportion as love is stronger —that, if God is love, there must be eternal sacrifice in Him—and that we cannot dwell in love without partaking of that sacrifice.

Brethren, the process of discovering that earthly joys are all inadequate is only the method in which that sacrifice is sooner or later asked of all of you. And if any of you are tempted to shrink from making this sacrifice of the things of earth because you have lost or are losing your belief in the reality of One behind them to reciprocate your love, and take their place when they are gone, remember that the last love is the love that looks not for reciprocation ; and resolve still to dwell in love,—the love of the brethren, the love of the fatherless and widow in their afflictions, and you shall find at the last· that you have recreated the hope that you had lost—and know, with that spiritual knowledge that passeth understanding, that God IS because Love IS and God IS Love.

XI.
GATHERING OF FRAGMENTS.

"Gather up the fragments that remain, that nothing be lost."
ST. JOHN vi. 12.

THE words of the Word are eternal, and of infinite significance. Their meaning is not exhausted by the occasion that gave them birth. Unlike our half-hearted human sayings, that pass and are forgotten, the words of the Word are borne up from the far eternity and echo on into the far eternity, and the occasion of their utterance within the sphere of human history is only one among a thousand, to which they equally apply. For they come from Him who is the same yesterday, to-day, and for ever, and with whom there is no variableness, neither shadow of turning.

"Gather up the fragments that remain, that

nothing be lost." They carry us back to the unknown day when the earth was without form and void, and God out of its ruined fragments fashioned the universe anew; through the long ages when He treasured up the wasted seeds of the primeval forests, to give warmth, and light, and life, and power to a race that was not yet born, and committed the bodies of His creatures, as they passed away after their kind, to the safe keeping of their rocky sepulchres, that man in after time might gather from them new knowledge of the ways of his Creator; and on into the distant future when the world shall have passed away, but that Word which passeth not away shall have gathered together into one the children of God scattered abroad, of those whom God has given Him losing none. They express an attribute of the divine nature, a law of the divine mind, an eternal principle of the divine action, and therefore, when they appeal as an injunction to ourselves, we can obey them in the full assurance that they are no mere accommodation to our weakness, casual in its origin, and therefore uncertain in fulfilment, but part and parcel of the one great method by which our Father has worked hitherto, and by which therefore, in our case also, he will work.

Brethren, it is in this assurance that I would ask you to recall the words to-night, and, as another Christian year is ending, to gather up the fragments that remain. For another year is over, and we have but fragments of time left to us, fragments few and frail as the autumn leaves upon our trees. Seventy years are few enough for the work we have to do, but fifty are the lifetime of an ordinary man; and in these days of great catastrophes, and accidents, and illnesses, who is there that can venture to call fifty years his own? And even such a fragmentary time as still remains to us may never bring again to us one tithe of the opportunities which we have lavishly, regardlessly, squandered in the past. The time behind us is like a garden in its luxuriance of opportunities—opportunities of culture, opportunities of holiness, opportunities of prayerfulness, opportunities for loving our neighbour, opportunities for knowing our God. But the time before us, however long, may be in comparison a desert, with its solitudes only broken by a few oases here and there. Nor is this all; time and opportunity do not leave us where they found us. Each hour wasted, each opportunity neglected, weakens our power of using the remnant that is left. Think of the health and strength which sloth, intemperance, impurity, have sapped and undermined till only their fragments still remain. Think of the powers of intellect which might have been ours had we developed them, but which we have stunted, stifled, stupefied, till we have shut ourselves out from the great world of thought. Think of our childhood's capacity for saintliness, and the habits, the virtues, the graces, which might by this time have been ours; and then, as you look forward again to the shortness of the time remaining, remember that its shortness is yet further shortened by the fact that all your capacities, your body, your mind, your spirit, are now only the fragments of their former selves; and "gather up the fragments that remain, that nothing be lost."

It is an hard task—a task which at first sight may well dizzy and appal us—a task from which many a soul has shrunk back again into hopelessness, crying as he sank beneath the wave of custom the awful cry, "It is too late." But there are two thoughts to give us courage and cheer us onward to the work—the thought that we are working on the lines which our God has Himself laid down for us,.and the thought that we are following where others, age by age, have gone before. Recall for a moment, when you are tempted to give up gathering the fragments, how fruitful, how triumphant, in the Bible and in all past history, the fragmentary lives of penitence have been. Remember David and all his trouble; how, in the very midst of his kingly career, he would seem, in human estimation, to have undone the work of a lifetime; to have set his people, and he their shepherd, a public example of the two greatest social sins; to have forfeited his royal power into the hands of an unscrupulous servant; and to have called the destroying angel down upon his people. If ever a king could be said to have reduced his life's work to fragments, it is David. And yet, to take only one single instance out of others, from the agonies of penitence with which the thought inspired him, came that great psalm, which now for near three thousand years has cheered, and sustained, and comforted, the sorrowing, suffering sons of men, and made it possible to them to offer the broken fragments of their lives to God. Or, again, remember Jonah, how with the burden of the souls of all great Nineveh upon his conscience he takes flight, and while he is flying the sinful people are being called, unready, disappointed, to their account; till he comes back, and even then unwillingly, to face only the remaining fragment of those to whom he had at first been sent; but the thought raises his whole nature to a white heat of penitential power, which invests his words with a superhuman, a miraculous capacity, to turn all sinful Nineveh, in a few days, to repentance. Or, pass again to the New Testament and the lives of penitence recorded there. Picture to yourselves Mary Magdalene in the days of her conversion, and the thoughts of all the shame and sorrow, and wasted womanhood of her bygone days. And yet, as the result of it all, she is privileged, above other women, to be near, and to attend upon Him whom kings and prophets, age after age, had desired to see and had not seen, till, when Jesus was risen early the first day of the week, we read that He appeared first to Mary Magdalene, out of whom He had cast seven devils. Or think of the high promises lavished, the high hopes centred, upon St. Peter,—that he should be a rock, a pillar, a tower of strength to support the weakness of his brethren,—and yet, in a moment of weakness, he turns round upon his destiny, throws it all away, crushes it all to fragments; he whose name and vocation was to be a corner-stone, becomes a reed shaken with the wind. It is done, it is gone, it is over, and there are only left a few bitter tears. And yet, from those tears he rises to feed the flock of Christ, to be a pillar of the Church, and to merit, after a few years' labour, a glorious death of martyrdom. Once more, recall the prince of penitents, St.

Paul, as he retired into the Arabian desert to contrast his future with his past. Suddenly, in mid-life, with only half his years remaining, he is called upon to abandon all he had lived for in the past,—to look back upon all his Pharisaic learning, his religious enthusiasm, his social reputation, all that he had laboriously worked for in the past, as useless, or worse than useless, —and to cast it all away, and to consecrate the remaining fragments of his lifetime to the counteraction of all which he was most fitted to uphold. And as if this were not enough, he is checked, and hampered, and hindered at every turn. He is scourged, he is stoned, he is thrown to beasts, he is shipwrecked, he is paralysed—amid this open violence—by the fear of secret assassination. And through all this, he is for ever wrestling with terrible temptation, and yet forced to work with patience to obtain his daily bread. The whole life, as we look into it, breaks up into a few fragments,— scattered sermons, scattered letters, scattered residence in fifty cities, broken up and interfered with by voyages, and imprisonment, and shattered health. And yet, out of those gathered fragments, God all the while was fashioning the life, and the doctrine, and the discipline which was for ages to control the world,—till men have even found it possible to say now, after eighteen centuries, that the true founder of Christianity was St. Paul.

And above and beyond even these, in the startlingness of his example, stands the man who, in his dying moment, when time for repentance seemed past and over, gathered up the fragments of a lifetime by the intensity of one aspiration, and is to-day with Christ for ever in the Paradise of God.

Such are a few of the great Scriptural gatherers of fragments, and thousands upon thousands, age after age, have taken courage from their example to follow in their steps. And if only we could look into the secret things of Christian history, and see the mainspring of the lives of many a one of its greatest heroes,—of the great missionaries who left all to preach the Gospel in unknown, barbaric lands; of the founders and leaders of those great orders, brotherhoods, societies, which handed on the light of Christ through the dark ages of the world; of the builders of our great cathedrals, and the loving artists that adorned them; of all the great teachers, and preachers, and benefactors of their brethren; and of a myriad fameless, nameless ones, who are now among the multitude that no man can number, —we could trace all their heroic energy to a day when they had looked upon their past lives, and seen there only scattered fragments, and, startled at the sight, resolved to gather the remainder together, that nothing might be lost.

But if we would gather up our fragments we must work by the two methods which were the secrets of all the fruitfulness of the fragmentary lives of old,—humility and prayerfulness.

You are familiar with the story of the Roman king to whom a wise woman came and offered nine books of sacred prophecy, to be bought for a great price. The king refused her, and she went away and cast three of the volumes in the fire, and then came back to ask him the same price for the remainder. Again she was dismissed with scorn, and came back with only three remaining, for which she still demanded the same great price. But at last the king had learnt the lesson, and bowed his Roman pride to buy the fragmentary treasure for what might once have given him the whole. And it is so that we ourselves must act. We are often apt to think and speak as if the very notion that we can, with impunity, after squandering all the wealth that God has given us, offer Him, as if in mockery, the few last farthings that remain, were an insult and a degradation to the character of God. But if you will analyse the thought, you will see that the real basis of the feeling is not your fear of dishonouring God, but your fear of lowering the contemptible dignity of man. If you were still able to do some great thing for God you would perhaps condescend to do it; but only to wash seven times in Jordan is too little a thing for your pride. But in this very fact, my brethren, the value of penitence consists. For humility

is the especial Christian virtue, it is the
especial quality in the Incarnation which fills
us with astonishment; and from the moment
of the Incarnation it has been the one characteristic that has distinguished the Christian
from all other lives. And the reason which
has made humility such a fruitful source of
spiritual strength is, that it clears the ground,
and makes a secure foundation possible. It
blows away the clouds of our self-conceit, it
scatters the debris of our former lives, and digs
down through the shifting sands, and rottenness,
and nothingness of self, till at last it has laid
bare the rock, and found that that rock is
Christ. It makes a man cease from comparing
himself with the actions and characters of other
men, and forces home upon him the importunate
question, "What hast thou that thou hast not
received?" and that question once pressed home
must, at whatever cost it be, wring out, unwillingly, the answer, Nothing, absolutely nothing,
—blank, dark, empty, unmeaning, impotent
nothingness. Not till he has given that answer does a man truly know himself. And the

secret of those great lives which we have been passing in review is, that they have been reared upon a basis of humility. You cannot look back upon your lost time, and opportunities, and faculties, and realise that what remains to you is but the fragment of a fragment, the shadow of a shade, and that all the efforts of your after lifetime can only rescue, at the most, the insignificant remnant of what would have been insignificant even as a whole, and not feel yourself humbled by the thought. "My soul is full of trouble, and my life draweth nigh unto hell. I am counted as one of them that go down into the pit, and I have been even as a man that hath no strength. I am so fast in prison that I cannot yet get forth. My sight faileth for very trouble; Lord, I have called daily upon Thee, I have stretched forth my hands unto thee. Dost Thou show wonders among the dead, or shall the dead rise up again and praise Thee? Shall Thy loving-kindness be shown in the grave, or Thy faithfulness in destruction? Shall Thy wondrous works be known in the dark; and Thy righteousness in the land where all things are forgotten?" "O, remember how short my time is; wherefore hast Thou made all men for nought?" Such is the Psalmist's feeling of his own unutterable nothingness; *but*, see how, by its very intensity, it forces him to prayer. That is why humility is so powerful a virtue. Because, by showing us our own nothingness, it forces us to depend on God; and the expression of that dependence is prayerfulness. Prayerfulness, brethren, means more than prayer, for it means prayer become an abiding principle of the life, a permanent attribute of the character, a perpetual state. It is possible to say stated prayers, at stated intervals, on stated days; and to be regular in morning and evening, and even in noonday devotion, and yet to be very far removed from the real life of prayer. Prayer has been defined to be a wish referred to God; and if we could keep this thought before us, it would help us to acquire the habit of prayer, by making us refer each wish, as it came into our minds, to God, for His assistance in furtherance or frustration. And the way to this is to practise short, informal, spontaneous prayer; ejaculatory, as it is called, from being darted arrow-like to heaven. We have examples of such prayer in the short sharp cries of our own Liturgy. "O God, make speed to save us!" "O God, make clean our hearts within us!" "O Son of David, have mercy upon us!" They ask for nothing; they expect no answer to come to us in a definite shape; they are simply inarticulate, cry-like, sob-like, intense upliftings of the heart to God; efforts to rise into an atmosphere where our spirits can breathe freely, sighs of the home-sick soul.

Brethren, it is by the gradual use of such short prayers on all occasions, bridging the intervals, and linking together the times of your more formal prayers, that you may both acquire, and discover in what degree you have acquired, that prayerfulness to which it is the object of humility to lead you, and which will alone enable you to gather up the fragments that remain.

Take, therefore, these thoughts home with you, as the year closes and the last leaves fall;

the thought that there remains even to the youngest of you, but a fragment, the thought that God has taught you by His example as well as by His Word, to gather up the fragments that remain, that nothing may be lost; the thought of the countless thousands, of like passions with yourselves, who have gathered up their fragments, to great and fruitful purpose; because the fewness of their fragments forced them to be humble, and humility forced them into prayer. And pray to-night that you too may so follow their good example, that when your Lord shall gather the fragments of your mortal bodies from the grave, He may deign also to accept the fragments of your spiritual life; and when the accuser shall ask mockingly, "What are they among so many?" may say, "Make the men sit down,"—sit down in the kingdom of God.

APPENDIX.

AMONG the many dangers consequent upon the increase of specialisation in our modern thought, there is perhaps none greater, because less obvious, than the unfair advantage afforded to negative and critical, as against dogmatic and positive opinion. For constructive and dogmatic systems must of necessity be many-sided, and liable, therefore, to the criticism of a thousand different specialists, who gain, or seem to gain, advantages in their several departments, and then, by accepting each other's results without the comprehension of each other's methods, assume that there is a cumulative improbability against the system they attack. But on examination it will often be found that such special arguments prove too much, and are less destructive of their common opponent than of each other. Instead of being various applications of one system of thought in different regions of inquiry, they turn out to rest on totally different foundations, to belong to utterly different schools of philosophy, to be, if we bring them together, mutually exclusive of one another, and to form in fact not a cumulus, but a residuum of argument, which derives its only plausibility from the fact that it can never all be viewed at once. It is like the evil spirit in the Eastern fairy tale—changing its shape as we change our weapons; now a lion, then an insect, then a bird, then a flame, then a cloud. Meanwhile the dogmatic attitude, reactionary and obscurantist as it may seem, may really after all be due to a superior insight into the controversial exigencies of the situation, and a wider acquaintance with the history of thought. Truth has grown from age to age, by action and reaction, out of the harmony of opposites. It is a familiar sight in politics to watch half-truths pressed beyond their limits, till in turn they become falsehoods, and a reaction is provoked; and the same process is for ever at work in the intellectual world. A philosopher proclaims a new truth, and knows the while that it is but a fragment; but his followers soon invest it with an artificial completeness and finality, and imagine it the key to all their locks, till at last the truth is too strong for them, and bears witness to its own finitude—refuses to be worshipped—refuses to be misrepresented, and after oscillating awhile in the breath of popular favour, settles into place; an important contribution, it may be, to the development of human thought, but very far from what men prophesied in the first flush of its golden appearing. A Christian, therefore, is fairly entitled to consider that "divide et impera" is as sound a motto for defence as for attack, and that a dogmatic system which has already outlived more than one philosophic opponent, may yet survive those modern attacks whose supposed unity of character is only the abstract unity of their agreement in a common negation, the unity by which Pilate and Herod were made friends; while a further examination of the nature of these attacks might confirm him in the wisdom of this attitude by showing him that they are not scientific, but philosophic in their origin; not, that is to say, new facts, which modern science has discovered, but old theories which have been read into those facts; theories at least as old as Christianity itself, and theories whose rejection from time to time by all the greatest philosophic names, affords some presumption at least of their improbability.

For example, the chief characteristic of our modern ways of thinking is our use of the comparative method, and our consequent interest in the category of evolution or development. Instead of looking at things in isolation, and making every science a separate monograph, we now view them in the light reflected from their history and context, as parts of one great, articulate, concatenated whole; and nothing is independent, and all things live by a borrowed life, and the farthest parts of the wide universe are seen to be members one of another. We study the world embryologically, and trace the law of its life through its gradual increase of specification, of definiteness, of complexity —what was potential becoming actual, the nebula a world, the cell an organism, the variety a species, the village community a nation, the myth a philosophy, the instinct a religion—while through it all the remnants of the old still linger to beautify the new, making a picture where the central colour is present everywhere subduedly; a harmony where a few simple notes are again caught up and again, and echoed in a thousand new and ever newer applications. All this is scientific fact, and nowhere has it more fruitful results than in the regions of theology and morals; but by impressing the category of "development" or "becoming" too exclusively upon the imagination, the comparative method has tended to obscure the no less important category of "identity" or "being," the fact that, in Butler's language, "Things are what they are, and their consequences will be what they will be." In other words, because we see that all things are related, we have come to think that they are only relative, or, as the phrase goes, " constituted by the sum of their relations," without separate identity or nature of their own.

Colour and sound and heat are but modes of molecular motion, and may be formulated in terms of motion. Flowers are transfigured sunbeams, and organic life a refined mechanism, and thought a function of phosphorus, and great men the creations of their age. This intimate correlation of things and forces in their varying moods is not only a scientific fact, but a fact of fascinating interest; but the further inference that each thing and force has not its own peculiar individuality is nothing more than a mere fiction of the imagination. We cannot make a flower by concentrating sunbeams, or life by the rearrangement of carbon and phosphorus and lime, or genius by a judicious system of competitive examination. Water may be only a combination of oxygen and hydrogen, but you cannot drown yourself in the one, or slake your thirst with the other, or make either support your ships. In each case something has evaporated from the crucible of the analyst, and we only discover its presence when it is for ever past recall; and yet it was just that something which held the elements together, and gave them their identity, their reality, their nature, making them an *unity*, and not merely a *sum*.

It is of great importance, therefore, that we should separate in our minds the comparative method, and the theory of evolution to which it has led, from this false philosophy of relativity by which they have been perverted. The two former are, to all practical intent, strictly modern contributions to the world of thought, while the latter is only a revived survival of the Greek sophists, and of the Renaissance, and generally of those periods of "illumination" in which novelties are numerous, and the fluency more conspicuous than the fixity of things. And it is not therefore altogether unnatural that it should be the popular philosophy of the present day. Art, we are told, is no longer "eternity looking through time," but a casual coincidence of picturesque attitudes and situations, passing with the passage of the moment that gave them birth, and owing their origin to time and climate, and national character and circumstance— Turner to the northern mists, and Titian to the southern sun. In politics, too, and social science, it is the philosophy of relativity alone which can justify and make possible the violation of the notion of personality, *i.e.* of personal identity, which is practically involved in so much that is now said and written against property and liberty of bequest, and the distinct duties and prerogatives of the sexes, and indeed against all observation of degree, priority, and place.

Then in morals, utilitarianism is the fashionable creed; not the nobly spurious utilitarianism of Austin, which makes utility an index of the moral law, but the consistent appeal to utility as the ultimate principle of conduct, whether international, public, or personal; and utilitarianism is merely another name for relativity in action.

Religions, too, in the same way, are viewed as relative to their age and nation, and as being all equally true for their adherents, because equally resulting from the national culture, whether primitive or advanced. A higher religion may naturally follow as the appendix to a higher civilisation, but to enforce it by missionary effort and out of its context would be absurd.

And beyond all these theories—and far wider spread than any of them, though flowing from the combination of them all—is that fatal *relativity in life* which is now so common; the substitution of an appreciative sympathy with all the moods of life and action for the personal practice of any one; the acquiescence in the besetting tendency of all literary ages to feel everything and be nothing, and under the specious names of "culture" and "criticism," to glory in their shame. The few mean it, and the many echo it, more or less unconsciously, in aimless, unmeaning lives, without earnestness, without identity, without practical belief in any reality at all.

In fact, the philosophy of relativity is everywhere around us, and even if not consciously accepted, it taints the air men breathe, and secretly modifies first their instincts, and then their opinions, and at last their beliefs. Men indulge it in art, till unawares it has sapped their morals; or dream of it in politics, and either wake to find they have no religion, or are driven to reiterate the worn-out falsehood, that one thing may be true in philosophy and another in faith, as if it were possible in this age of consequence for men to be saved by their inconsistency from the ruin which their opinions ought in fairness to entail.

And the consequence of all this is that the philosophy of relativity has been allowed to interpret all the scientific facts with which the comparative method has of late enriched us, exclusively in its own interest, and then to appeal to them in support of itself. For, if things are essentially constituted by the sum of their relations in the sense understood by that philosophy, *i.e.* without nucleus of self-identity, metaphysical or physical, inherent or derived, it must follow that there is no such thing as reason or spirit in the universe, for reason and spirit involve the notion of something permanently self-identical and independent; and without reason and spirit there can be no first or final cause, or, in other words, no conscious intention connecting the stages of the world's development, and the whole aspect of natural science will be altered. For example, the existence of rudimentary organs, which are useless in the place of their occurrence, and only blossom into usefulness in after ages or higher races, as well as the dwarfed survivals, in civilised humanity, of structures which were only useful to the savage or the brute, are, in their appeal to our sense of beauty, as .strong an evidence of "design" as could ever have been furnished by an appeal to our use. Like the shadows in a picture passing into light, or the rising and the falling of cadences in music, their 'gradation binds the world together into one great work of art, and sets us wondering that so much melody can be brought from so few notes. But deny the existence of reason, with the philosophy of relativity, and these very facts can at once be turned into additional proofs that nature is irrational and impotent, since, if wisdom and power had framed the universe, we should see none of these half-hewn blocks, none of these marks of the chisel, or unseemly fragments left littering the workshop. The planets would have moved in circles, and the lenses of the eye been true, and the human race would have sprung into being, "a grand democracy of forest trees."

The religious and moral phenomena of the world can then be explained upon the same hypothesis, as evolved in the conflict of forces from the primitive elements of things. The belief in spiritual existence is due to more or less complex inference from the apparitions—the purely physical apparitions of our dreams; while the utility or harm of actions to the stronger savage or the stronger clan, soon leads to their classification as praiseworthy or the reverse. We have here the germ of moral as well as of religious consciousness; and these in the course of ages interacting upon one another, we find morals enforced by religious sanctions, and so the beginnings of ecclesiasticism, and orthodoxy in turn made a moral question, and theology evolved. From this point the subsequent development of religions can be easily traced by help of the survivals embedded broadcast in the strata of history or savage culture. The Trinity is proved to be a mere development, because its imperfect analogue has been fortunately preserved to us in Egypt and in India; and the

Incarnation is a fable, for eight such stories are told of Vishnoo; and the Christian symbols are only relics of the coarse nature-worships of the early world; and the Christian priesthood, and the Christian ritual, and the Christian sacraments are all unreal, because other religions have priesthoods, and a ritual, and sacraments.

Now this account of the evolutionary origin of morals and religion is so symmetrical, so intelligible, so in harmony with every fresh generalisation of the day, as to throw a paralysing fascination even over those who would wish things otherwise, and many who shrink from the open atheism which is logically its consequence, go so far with it as at least to relinquish all definite forms of belief. But this danger would hardly occur if men were more accustomed to distinguish between the regions of fact and hypothesis, of philosophy and science.

For men would then be able to separate, in what is vaguely called the theory of evolution, the element of scientific truth from the element of philosophic fallacy, and to judge the latter upon its merits in the light of the history of thought. A recurrence to that history would remind them that the sophistic philosophy of relativity was, as we have seen, no new appearance in the world of thought, and that, though fresh facts have from time to time been pressed into its service, they have been coloured by the theory in question before they could be used in its support; while Plato and

Aristotle, in their opposition to it, were led into modes of thinking which were lineally ancestral of the Christian doctrine of the Trinity. That doctrine, in its intellectual aspect, as elaborated in the first three Christian centuries, may fairly be called the last word of Greek speculation, and it may be reassuring to many minds amid present difficulties to remember that the fundamental doctrine of their faith is not an incomprehensible mystery to which rational philosophy is diametrically opposed, but the legitimate development, under Hebrew and Christian influence, of the only philosophy which the greatest intellects of the most intellectual of our race judged adequate to solve the mystery of this unintelligible world. For philosophy has been well described by a modern French philosopher as "the incessant effort of the human spirit after rest;" and if rest is to be attained, it must be in the reduction of all things to an unity, for "the double-minded man is unstable," and dualism is philosophic failure. Unity, in order to rest, has been the aim of all philosophical endeavour, from that of prehistoric India to that of the present day; and yet, after all these centuries of searching, the unity seems still unfound, the dualism still more emphatic; for it has been shown, after much analysis, to be rooted and grounded in the very nature of our being—to be the condition of our personality. When thought was young, and the first philosophers set out upon their search for unity, they were too ignorant of what they wanted to be hopeless. The variety of the world, as it seemed, was something outside them, which they could easily gather together into one. And for a while each successive simplification would feed hope. But time has gone on, and analogy, and connection, and identity have been traced everywhere, and stars, and forces, and forms of life are known in their intimate relationship; and yet the dualism, the ultimate dualism, so far from solution, has been intensified, for we have found that it is not without us but within. The sickness that we had hoped to remedy is discovered to be our own, and the dying physician cannot heal himself. And so with long failure we have learned humility, and philosophy is narrowed to psychology, the study of the universe to the study of the human mind. Personality, and the personal consciousness which the course of philosophy and the various incidents of our historical development have thus gradually emphasised, is for us the necessary point of all philosophical departure. Our present problem, therefore, is how to solve the dualism involved in our personal consciousness, or, failing that, to see in what direction a solution may be hoped for. And on facing this problem we notice (1) that the dualism between ourselves and all that we are not, but desire to feel, and to know, and to be—between subject and object, as we call it—is a fact of ordinary consciousness, resting, *i.e.*, upon the same authority that makes our thinking possible, and incapable by consistent thinkers of being explained away; (2) that the two elements of this dualism—the subjective and the objective factor—are, on the same testimony, equally primitive, equally real. Neither can be used as a fulcrum for removing the other, without contradiction of the facts of consciousness, *i.e.* of the possibility of all sane thinking; (3) that these two elements stand over against each other, like opposite mirrors—the farther we look into the one, the farther we see into the other—the more we separate them in one aspect, the more in another we unite them. If, for instance, by a highly imaginative effort of abstraction, we regard the universe as merely material and chaotic, the self that is within will be chaotic and material too. The separation between us and the world would be merely the local difference between two groups of atoms fringing off into one another; while our union, which at first sight might appear intimate, would in reality be imperfect, limited, external—the union of atoms in juxtaposition which only appear to touch. But endow the supposed self with sense, and you immediately endow its corresponding object with sensibility. The two at once start asunder; they are no longer identical in kind, like the inorganic atoms, but for that very reason they are in more intimate connection than that of mechanical juxtaposition, or even of chemical combination. But as we look deeper and see that the sensitive self is also intellectual, new light is thrown upon the external order, and that becomes intelligible, and while thought and its object are far wider apart than are sense and the object of sensation, they are capable of a proportionately subtler union, because of one which is neither external nor limited by space or time. Finally, when we know ourselves to be not only sensitive and rational, but also personal, we become aware that there is a whole universe of personality outside us, while as persons we remain infinitely, utterly alone—cut off from the impersonal nature below us, the sunsets and the flowers and the mountains that we cannot mingle with and be lost in; cut off from the human persons about us, that can never know us, or we them; cut off from the Personality beyond us, that can never love us, or we Him. The dualism has reached a climax; distinction has passed into division, division into separation, separation into alienation.

"Is He not all but thou, that hast power to feel, I am I?"

Yet through the severance, and because of the severance effected by personality, a higher form of unity has become possible — the interpenetration of soul by soul, identity of thought, identity of action, love. Such are the results of our psychological analysis; a dualism both of whose factors are equally primitive and real, and whose solution, demanded with agony, becomes gradually more conceivable as we advance in the scale of being from the atom to the man. And on comparing these facts with the history of philosophy, we find the four possible modes of treating them have all in turn been tried; systems which, like that of Porphyry, suppose a primitive indifference underlying and more abstract than the elemental atoms of the universe, and having made this solitude, miscall it peace; atheistic systems of materialism which suppress one side of the dualism; pantheistic systems of idealism which equally suppress the other, both alike purchasing unity at the cost of their veracity, and claiming to satisfy the cravings of consciousness by the denial of their existence; and lastly, philosophies which, from Aristotle downward, have preferred veracity to system, and recognised the dualism at the risk of being charged with failure. In other words, the only philosophy which can stand the test of facts confesses the solution of its problem to be still in the future, still to seek, and perhaps even for ever unattainable. In the face, therefore, of the proved unveracity of the three former systems, and the confessed insufficiency of the fourth, we may fairly welcome any other hypothesis which will throw light upon the question. Such an hypothesis is the Christian dogma of the Trinity in unity, which accords accurately with all the natural analogies that we have been reviewing; for it shows the dualism of personality to be solved not by its mutilation, but by its intensification in an infinite personal subject which, as infinite, must have an adequate, and therefore a personal object, to which object it must be united not by an abstract or single relation, such as exists between thought or love, and their respective objects among ourselves, but by a relation which is adequate, including all possible relations, and therefore perfect and therefore personal. Heighten the elements of the dualism to infinity, and it is solved.

The Christian doctrine of the Trinity, therefore, though it cannot be pictured to the imagination, is at least in striking harmony with all the analogies of things; and while it preserves the divine transcendence which gives fixity to all relative existence without sacrificing the divine immanence which makes life and progress possible, it is the only form of theism which cannot be called anthropomorphic; for the very possibility as a conception of Triune personality has been denied, and the same idea cannot in fairness be called anthropomorphic and inconceivable.

And with the restoration of this doctrine to its place, instead of the philosophy of relativity, a teleological view of nature will again be possible, and the whole history of the world's evolution will assume a new significance, as moving to one far-off divine event, of which the Incarnation is at once an anticipation and a prophecy.

i. Science has brought into quite new prominence the *reality* of matter, and that especially as an integral part of our human personality. It has traced impressions from the world of matter, as they are telegraphed along the nerves and photographed within the brain, to be reproduced in our thoughts and emotions, and to give their character to our whole being; and, sweeping away the faded metaphors of old-world idealisms about the body being a prison, or a garment, or an instrument, has declared boldly that the blood is the life. The Incarnation is not only consistent with such a view, but even demands it—as the finer theological instinct of earlier days was well aware; and in the deepest sense we are materialists from the very fact that we are Christians. For the counter-agent of materialism is not idealism, but sacramentalism.

ii. Science has acquired a new *dignity* for matter by the exhibition of its intimacy with spirit. The loveliness of its forms and colours, the wonder of its versatility, the mystery of its strange sympathies and antipathies, are for ever haunting us with the suggestion that matter is not what it seems. But such suggestions have been long anticipated and confirmed by the sacramental system, in whose light we see the material order to be another aspect only of the spiritual, which is gradually revealing itself through material concealment, in the greater and the lesser Christian sacraments which radiate from the Incarnation, and in all the types, and parables, and symbolisms of nature, and the sacraments of storm and calm, and of the sunset and of the star-rise, and in every flash of an eye, or flush of a cheek, or pulse of a hand, that is, in its degree, the material instrument of spiritual communion. And so

> "The whole round world is every way
> Bound with gold chains about the feet of God."

iii. Science speaks of a *destined* perfectibility for matter. For the law of the material universe is one of ever-quickening development. The impenetrable atoms in combination lose their stubbornness, and melt into varying moods of light and heat and electricity, binding the universe together with a delicate network of sensitive nerves; and the self-same chemical elements that in their deadness make the mountains, inform the life of the trees that clothe them, and the motions of the beasts that haunt them, and the senses and hearts and brains of the men that look upon them and love them. The atoms are refined, transfigured, glorified from rigid obedience to willing freedom, but still they are the atoms. And inspired by such a past, science prophesies for matter an indefinite, infinite increase, of perfection in the time to come. Theology consecrates the prophecy, and shows matter in mediæval language, "subtle," "agile," and "impassible," and "glorious," sharing the throne of heaven. The music is not less material than was the sculpture, because it is more spiritual, nor the vision through a glass darkly more material than the vision face to face. And as we look back, in the light of the Incarnation, upon the long dim vista of the world's material development, there is new meaning for us in the old language—" A body have I prepared for thee ;" and a new hope in our looking for the resurrection of the dead.

THE END.

Printed by R. & R. CLARK, *Edinburgh*

www.ingramcontent.com/pod-product-compliance
Lightning Source LLC
Chambersburg PA
CBHW032151160426
43197CB00008B/870